The Poetry of Thomas Kinsella

Maurice Harmon

This critical introduction to the poetry of Thomas Kinsella provides the reader and student with a sensitive analysis of the poet's achievement and a workbook through which a fuller understanding of individual poems and their interrelationships can be obtained. Kinsella's poetry in part reflects an inheritance of oppressive social conditions, and impoverished literary scene and a feeling of precariousness in modern life. It is a constant exploration of suffering, love, death; of the artistic act; and of personality and myth. It is a seeking for an ongoing creative response to experience. Dr Harmon's study is a critical appraisal and interpretation of the poet's thematic concerns and sensibilities. It illumines a great many of the dark complexities of Kinsella's tragic vision and brings to us, poem by poem, a rich appreciation of the poet's art.

Maurice Harmon, a graduate of Harvard, is a lecturer in English at University College, Dublin, and Editor of the *Irish University Review: A Journal of Irish Studies.* He has taught Anglo-Irish literature at Harvard, Notre Dame and Ohio State universities and in Europe at the Sorbonne and the universities of Basle, Berne and Zurich. He is a member of the American Committee for Irish Studies and of the International Association for the Study of Anglo-Irish Literature. Among his published works are *Sean O'Faolain: a critical introduction, Modern Irish Literature, 1800-1967* and *J. M. Synge Centenary Essays, 1971.*

Jacket illustration adapted from a brush drawing by Louis Le Brocquy published in *The Táin* by the Dolmen Press. By kind permission.

HUMANITIES PRESS

The Poetry of Thomas Kinsella

By the same author

Sean O'Faolain: a critical introduction. University of Notre Dame Press (Notre Dame and London, 1967)

Modern Irish Literature, 1800-1967. A Reader's Guide. Dolmen and Oxford University Press (1967). Dufour, Pa (1968).

Fenians and Fenianism. Centenary Essays, ed., Scepter (Dublin, 1968). University of Washington (Seattle, 1969)

The Celtic Master. Being Contributions to the First James Joyce Symposium in Dublin, ed., Dolmen and Oxford (1969), Dufour (1970)

J.M. Synge Centenary Papers 1971. Dolmen and Oxford (1972), Humanities Press (New York, 1972).

Malone Shakespeare, ed., *King Richard II, Romeo and Juliet, King Lear, Coriolanus.* Longman, Brown and Nolan (1970-72)

The Poetry of Thomas Kinsella
'With darkness for a nest'

Maurice Harmon

HUMANITIES PRESS

ATLANTIC HIGHLANDS, N.J.

First published in the U.S.A. 1975
by Humanities Press
Atlantic Highlands, N.J. 07716
by arrangement with Wolfhound Press of Dublin

Library of Congress Cataloging in Publication Data

Harmon, Maurice.
  The poetry of Thomas Kinsella.

  Bibliography: p.
  Includes index.
  1. Kinsella, Thomas--Criticism and interpretation.
PR6021.I35Z7 1975   821'.9'14   75-9875
ISBN 0-391-00366-0
ISBN 0-391-00387-9 pbk.

Printed in the United States of America

CONTENTS

Quotations from the works of Thomas Kinsella
are reproduced by kind permission of
Mr Kinsella and the Dolmen Press

INTRODUCTION

'I wrote my first poem, when I was eighteen, out of curiosity; my second, at twenty, as a joke. The third was written soon after with a faint foreboding. When I write now, it is with feelings like those of the Redemptorist preacher's sparrow, which so foolishly devoted itself to the task of transporting to an unknown destination, grain by grain, and for a reason it could scarcely grasp, the sands of the sea.'

Thomas Kinsella

The decline in the volume and in the quality of Irish literature which became apparent in the thirties continued into the forties and early fifties. Yet it was in the inauspicious years of the late forties that Thomas Kinsella wrote his first poems. At that time only two poets of distinction were at work, both of an older generation, and neither offering him much in the way of subject matter or technique. Austin Clarke's best work had struggled with the problem of religious guilt and he had tended to isolate himself as a poet. Patrick Kavanagh wrote mainly of life on a small farm, a subject of no particular relevance for Kinsella. He was one of a small group of writers to emerge in the fifties and sixties which included the poets John Montague and Richard Murphy, and the novelists Aidan Higgins, John McGahern and Richard Power. All had been born about 1930 and had grown up in the Ireland that Sean O'Faolain, Frank O'Connor and Austin Clarke had found restrictive and uncongenial. But they belonged to a new generation and lived at a time when there were profound changes in the direction and in the quality of Irish life, when the country became less isolationist and adopted a less censorial attitude to life and letters. More cosmopolitan than their predecessors, they felt not only that

7

they belonged to a more liberal Ireland, but that they were part of, or could at least aspire to, the universal community of writers.

And so, to find themselves, they went abroad—to England, Europe, Africa or America. Kinsella, however, remained in Dublin, living for an important period of his imaginative and intellectual growth in a room in Baggot Street. His contemporaries produced work that reflected their overseas experience: Richard Murphy's *Archaeology of Love* (1955) is steeped in Mediterranean and classical culture, Montague's *Forms of Exile* (1958) is set mainly away from Ireland, Aidan Higgins's *Felo De Se* (1960) has several European settings, but Kinsella's *Another September* (1958) is universal in its themes, as though he would consume the entire combustible world in that room in Baggot Street.

When he and John Montague edited the *Dolmen Miscellany of Irish Writing* (1962), for by then it was clear that a significant number of new writers were at work, they made it clear that the writers included in the miscellany did not form 'any sort of movement' and that, while they did reflect a general change of sensibility, the main link between them was their 'obvious desire to avoid the forms of "Irishism"... so profitably exploited in the past'. Their search for literary models, as for experience of life, outside Ireland was part of their impulse to break free from Irish moulds.

Kinsella, like any young writer, worked at first with the aid of other poetic voices. There are Yeatsian influences in some of his early lyrics, particularly in the imagery and in the structure of his longer meditative poems, and he was strongly attracted to Auden whose ruminative lyrics he admired. The range of influences that may be detected in his work is indicative of his absorption in the task of becoming a poet, of learning his craft. He went to the German writers, Goethe, Heine, Maeterlinck and Hölderin, to old ballads and carols, to Old Irish material, to the seventeenth-century poets, Donne, Marvell and Crashaw, to the romantics, Keats and Wordsworth, to Matthew Arnold, and, of course, to the

8

moderns, to Pound, Yeats, Eliot, Auden, Lowell and, eventually, to the whole range of modern poetry.

All the new writers went abroad—in time Kinsella also broke free from his job in the Civil Service and went to America—but as time passed all have been drawn more and more to their own country, to their personal, familial and racial past, to places, people and events that link them physically and imaginatively with the patterns of life, the culture, that have helped to shape their minds and imaginations. Even to list some recent work is to illustrate how wide and definite this return has been: Aidan Higgins, *Langrishe, Go Down* (1966); Richard Murphy, *The Battle of Aughrim* (1968); John Montague, *The Rough Field* (1972); Thomas Kinsella, *Nightwalker and other poems* (1968). All of these works, and the list could be extended considerably, have in common a profoundly complex and personal exploration of the past. Informed by their contacts with literary developments abroad, the young writers are able to explore the Irish material in ways that are new and sometimes radical. In their hands Irish literature has been enriched and strengthened at a time when it seemed in danger of decay.

The fact that the Irish literary tradition was stronger in prose than in poetry at the time when Kinsella began to write was one reason for his search for models outside Ireland, although it must also be observed that the English tradition had much more to offer him. Another reason was the essentially universal nature of his thematic concerns which did not require the sanction or stimulus of a particular tradition and which in any case were not strongly or distinctively grounded in Irish literature. Speaking of his own work in 1966, he observed that his poems since 1956 had 'dealt with love, death and the artistic act; with persons and relationships, places and objects, seen against the world's processes of growth, maturing and extinction' (note 1). This part of his statement reiterates what he said in 1958 when *Another September* was published (note 2). What followed in the 1966 statement was directed more specifically to the work in *Downstream* (1962) and states his view of the human, including, most importantly, the artistic function. By that time he was, he said, increasingly concerned, in longer poems,

> with questions of value and order, seeing the human function (in so far as it is not simply to survive the ignominies of existence) as the eliciting of order from experience—the detection of the significant substance of our individual and common pasts and its translation imaginatively, scientifically, bodily, into an increasingly coherent and capacious entity; or the attempt to do this to the point of failure. (note 3)

More recently, in December 1967, commenting on the poems in *Nightwalker and other poems* (1968), he remarked that 'their subject in general is a developing view of life as an ordeal':

> The first two sections of the book begin with certain private experiences under the ordeal, and follow with celebrations of the countermoves—love, the artistic act—which mitigate the ordeal and make it fruitful, and even promise a bare possibility of order. The poems in the third section are about a few poets, and the function of poetry. In the last section the feeling reaches out to the Irish historical landscape and the 'new' Ireland, and inward to the imaginative hunger that (I believe) gives to existence whatever significance it may have. These poems are trying (as the whole book is) to find a balance in the violent zone, between the outer and the inner storms, where human life takes place. (note 4)

Like other tragic artists Kinsella responds to the destructive element, to the facts of suffering, erosion and death. These issues are part of his temperament and are only partly conscious. In his eyes men are 'all finally helpless in the service of a general brutality' (note 5). His characteristic terms are *brutal, squalid, ordeal, ignominies, failure* and *horror*. Opposed to them are his positive counter-terms—*order, honesty, acceptance, maturity, renewal, understanding* and *love*. Beginning with love lyrics cast in the sombre shadow of change and loss, his work carries him into deeper and more complicated investigations of the existential condition. Suffering is inquired into, made articulate and creatively appropriated or transmuted (note 6).

At the same time conditions in the Ireland of his youth intensified his tragic vision. The literary scene had been drastically diminished and the social environment was inimical to the exercise of the creative imagination. Writers of Sean O'Faolain's generation had struggled to achieve a balanced and detached relationship with a society which they found profoundly distasteful. Kinsella, who grew up in that society, has reflected its depressing and inhibiting influences in such poems as 'A Country Walk' and 'Nightwalker'.

But it was the effects of the Second World War that exacerbated his sense of the evil inherent in man. 'It was', he wrote, 'no news that the human mind was an abyss, and that the will, just as much as the imagination, was capable of every evil. But it was something new that in Nazi Germany creatures out of Hieronymus Bosch should have materialised into the world...' (note 7). The war, he felt, accelerated the 'process of disappointment' that had entered human life during the First World War. Its effect was to isolate the individual.

> The most sensitive individuals have been shaken loose from society into disorder, conscious of a numbness and dullness in themselves, a pain of dislocation and loss.... Everywhere in modern writing the stress is on personal versions of the world.... The detailed explorations of private miseries is an expedition into the interior to find out what may guide us in the future. It is out of ourselves and our wills that the

chaos came, and out of ourselves that some order must
be constructed.(note 8)
Oppressive social conditions, an impoverished literary scene
and a feeling of precariousness in modern life were but part
of Kinsella's inheritance. His isolation was also occasioned by
his sense of belonging to a tradition that was broken. When
he sought to identify his forebears he could only point to
Yeats and to the century of 'silence' that had preceded him.
Behind Yeats's Anglo-Irish tradition which he had made
meaningful there was a long native Irish tradition that Yeats
virtually had to ignore, despite his varied use of Gaelic
material. Kinsella's reflections on his own relationship with
the Irish past, delivered in 1966 at the annual meeting of the
Modern Language Association, are worth considering at some
length since they also help us to see how deep his sense of
isolation was. When he speaks of the 'air of continuity and
shared history' of former writers and dramatizes the dynamic
and confident sense of community and purpose available to
writers   at   former   periods,   he   indirectly   expresses   the
circumstances of his own 'great loss'. These must serve as a
backdrop to our study of his work, even though he has
almost made a virtue of the fact that he inherits a past that *is*
mutilated'.

> If I look deeper still in the need to identify myself,
> what I meet beyond the nineteenth century is a great
> cultural blur. I must exchange one language for
> another, my native English for eighteenth century Irish.
> After   the   dullness   of   the   nineteenth   century,
> eighteenth century Irish poetry is suddenly full of life:
> art in the service of real feeling—hatred for the foreign
> land-owner; fantasies and longings rising from the loss
> of an Irish civilization (the poets putting their trust in
> the Stuarts or the Spanish fleet or even the Pope of
> Rome); satires, love-songs, lamentations; outcries of
> religious fervour or repentance. And all of this in full
> voices, the voices of poets who expect to be heard and
> understood,   and   memorised—Eoghan   Ruadh   Ó

12

Súilleabháin, Donnchadh Ruadh MacConmara, Seán Clárach Mac Domhnaill, Tadhg Gaelach O Súilleabháin. They are the tragic end of Gaelic literature—but they are at home in their language; they have no more need to question the medium they write in than, say, John Clare writing in English.

Beyond them is the poet Aogán Ó Rathaille writing at the end of the seventeenth century and the beginning of the eighteenth. I am sure he is a major poet: the last great poet in Irish, and the last Irish poet, until Yeats, whose life can be seen as a true poetic career. It is a career that begins in the full light of Gaelic culture and ends in darkness, with the Gaelic aristocracy ruined and the death-blow already delivered to the Irish language.

Beyond O Rathaille, the course of Irish poetry stretches back for more than a thousand years, full of riches and variety: poetry as mystery and magic, in the earliest fragments and interpolated in the early sagas; poetry as instant, crystalline response to the world, in a unique body of nature lyrics; poetry as a useful profession—the repository of historical information and topography and custom; love poems and devotional poems of dignity and high technique; conventional bardic poetry heavy with tradition and craft. Here, in all this, I recognise simultaneously a great inheritance and a great loss. The inheritance is mine, but only at two enormous removes—across a century's silence, and through an exchange of worlds. The greatness of the loss is measured not only by the substance of Irish literature itself, but also by the intensity with which we know it was shared; it has an air of continuity and shared history which is precisely what is missing from Irish literature, in English or Irish, in the nineteenth century and today. (note 9)

None of this was available in Kinsella's own time. His fellow-writers he saw as 'a scattering of incoherent lives....

13

They can show me nothing about myself except that I am isolated' (note 10). That sense of isolation was fundamental. His instinct in *Another September* to dramatize events against a background of the transient was, he remarked,

> both the source of my poems and the reason for any lack of public concern which may be found in them. I find in practice that social or political matters, for example, or any motifs characteristic of a group, never arise; little is relevant but the dignity of the isolated person, whose conscious or unconscious bargainings with time insist, like those of a condemned or dying man, that they be respected. (note 11)

Ironically, Kinsella has done much to identify with the Old Irish period by his various translations of its poetry and prose (note 12), but in particular by his magnificent translation of its greatest product, the *Táin Bó Cuailnge*. Irish writers, noted for their concern with the issues of racial and cultural identity, have frequently turned to the past in search of a usable tradition; some, like Yeats, Synge, James Stephens and Austin Clarke, have found literary uses for myth, legend and folklore; many, like Lady Gregory, Frank O'Connor and Seán O'Faoláin, have acknowledged their connection with that past through translations and editions of its poems and stories. Kinsella's translation of the *Táin* and its related tales has suddenly made that past available to the English-speaking world. It is not part of the work of this study to assess the quality of the translation nor to discuss the literary merits of this prose-epic, but a few samples of its verse are given and briefly discussed in the penultimate chapter.

Kinsella decided to write in English rather than in Irish because it was the language he was bred in, because it offered him greater scope and because he believed that the Irish language was dying. In the end, he says, it was really not a matter of choice:

> for my own part I simply recognise that I stand on

one side of a great rift, and can feel the discontinuity in myself. It is a matter of people and place as well as of writing—of coming, so to speak, from a broken and uprooted family, of being drawn to those who share my origins and finding that we cannot share our lives (note 13).

Yeats, he argued, escaped from a similar isolation by creating a brief, select Anglo-Irish tradition. He turned away from his contemporary world 'to celebrate an old nobility at the end of the line'. But at least Yeats's isolation, unlike his own, was a conscious choice, a refusal to deal with the 'filthy modern tide'. It is because Joyce accepted the unattractive circumstances of modern life that Kinsella finds him more relevant to his own needs and interests.

Joyce's isolation is a mask. His relationship with the modern world is direct and intimate. He knows the filthy modern tide, and immerses himself in it.

He is, in Kinsella's estimation, 'the first major Irish voice to speak for Irish reality since the death of the Irish language' (note 14).

Thomas Kinsella's poetry comprises some of the most remarkable work to be produced in Ireland since the war. It reflects and is shaped by the experiences and attitudes of a distinctive generation within the Irish context, while at the same time transcending the merely local in its concerns with fundamental metaphysical issues and, most recently, in its use of psychic myth. In its apprehension of mutability and loss it takes up themes that have permeated English literature since Anglo-Saxon days. In its expression of horror at the new evidences of man's inherent capacities for evil it is part of a general literary consciousness in our time. But Kinsella does more than express horror and disappointment at the emergence of the great beast. At the basis of his response is a sense of possibility and expectation. What he has said about modern American poetry may be applied with equal, or even greater, validity to his own work: 'The scene has the groping characteristics of growth: multitudinous individual effort, frequent adjustments and failures, uncompleted movements; with an unusually high level of sensitiveness' (note 15). The difference between his barely possible dream, his qualified acceptance of Teilhard de Chardin's intuition about the nature of growth processes, and Yeats's concept of man as involved in a circumscribed treadmill of history, is worth noting. His view of this difference, like his view of his place in a broken tradition, must temper and guide our assessment of his work. The dominant impression to be gained from reading Yeats is, he has argued, that of 'progress towards some kind of triumph—a triumph of achievement, of absorption of poetic matter, or of understanding or acceptance' (note 16). Because of that tone of confidence it is the work of the younger poets and not of Yeats that provides 'the appropriate response to the experience of history as treadmill, a nightmare of returning disappointments' (note 17).

In his search for purpose and direction Kinsella has not been guided by religious or philosophical systems, nor does he, despite his close involvement with Irish mythology, make much use of the allusive method that provided Yeats and Eliot with a substantial framework for their sense of contemporary loss. He has remained essentially an isolated and personal poet intent on his own exploration of private miseries and the search for a meaningful pattern.

The attempts in this essay to investigate Kinsella's poetic achievement are introductory; more emphasis is placed on his thematic concerns than on his technical accomplishments. But his technical and linguistic skills are considerable, as is his ability to change pace in the long poems and to create a fruitful interplay between past and present within his general concept of continual movement towards extinction. There are important questions to be considered that are outside the scope of this essay, such as his handling of the idea of man and nature and how this relates to previous treatments of the same subject, particularly by the romantics. A poet of his stature inevitably raises questions of this kind. He needs to be 'placed' in relation to his contemporaries and within the perspectives of his own country. A study of recent Irish writing that would explore such subjects as history, nationalism, violence, love, individual freedom, in relation to their treatment by other Irish writers of this century would be immensely rewarding and useful (note 18). As for Kinsella's own work, there is the particular question of his textual revisions, specially in the case of 'Moralities', 'Downstream', the *Wormwood* poems and 'Nightwalker', for, as a glance at *Selected Poems 1956-1968* shows, he is the kind of poet who continually revises his work. The aim of this short study is simply to clarify his poetic concerns, to provide avenues of approach to his work and to suggest something about the nature of his achievement.

I gratefully acknowledge the generous help of Thomas Kinsella in its preparation, although he must not be held in any way responsible for its failings and omissions.

CHAPTER 1

ANOTHER SEPTEMBER (1958)

There are three kinds of poems in Thomas Kinsella's first major volume (note 1). One deals with the experience of love, another with such issues as space and time and their effects on the individual, and the third with the idea of a destructive element in the nature of things. Not that these three concerns can be separated; the celebration of love, for example, is often tinged with melancholy precisely because love itself and the lovers are subject to change, and poems that place humanity within the perspectives of time and space inevitably call attention to human littleness and impermanence.

Although the love lyrics spring from the experience of love, they are not so much tributes to a beloved's beauty or desirability as statements about the transforming power of love itself. She is invited to share in the wonder of which she is the source. For the young poet love is a challenge to expression: 'Love I consider a difficult, scrupulous art.' 'Per Imaginem', not in *Another September*, is given over almost completely to the problem of finding language adequate to the perceptions and responses that arise from love:

> Inaccessible softness of breast or voice in the dove
> Or high gull grace are what we are thinking of,
> The poise in quality of a bird.

The poem assembles images of dove, swan, bird and lake in a manner reminiscent of Yeats.

Indeed, as one would expect, many of these early poems

19

have echoes of other poets. 'Soft to your Places' hardly disguises its use of Auden and Yeats and might easily be dismissed as too imitative. But it is worth considering for what it reveals of Kinsella's attitude and poetic stance. It treats of love, ironically, as a present delight, a growing happiness, the 'difficulty' known to be part of it as yet only a 'fiction'. The speaker accepts the risks. Entertaining the idea that the growth of love may not proceed to perfection, he accepts the present for what it brings. The heart cannot see beyond and even the certainty of later change fails to restrain his ardent enjoyment of love. Indeed, the certainty of time's erosion intensifies present joy: 'I kiss/Because it is, because it is.'

The poem combines prayer and lament, the one for good luck, the other for the effects of mutability. The speaker is nicely poised between the two, tapping on wood to offset misfortune and enjoying love because he can, for the moment, keep time at a distance. He knows that things are not as 'simple' as he pretends: 'mighty work' produced even the common primrose and the lovers' easy discovery of love is deceptive. This agile positioning between happiness and regret, between love's intensities and time's future effects, is mimicked in the alteration from stanza and refrain between the larger movements of nature and the lovers' limited experience. The opposition between head and heart is gently and carefully relayed through the three main stanzas. The courage of that response is here lightly stressed as an instinctive reliance on the moment's achievements, but it pervades the style and diction of these love poems.

'Midsummer' has an accomplished grace of rhythm and rhyme and a playfulness of spirit (the echoes of Marvell are at least appropriate):

> Flowers whose names I do not know
> Make happy signals to us. O
>   Did ever bees
> Stumble on such quiet before!
> The evening is a huge closed door
>   And no one sees.

ANOTHER SEPTEMBER

In this celebration of a harmonious and beneficent
relationship between the lovers, creatures of the wood,
flowers and trees, the flowering of love is presented
metaphorically as a wondrous creature of the wood emerging
into view:

> Something that for this long year
> Had hid and halted like a deer
>   Turned marvellous,
> Parted the tragic grasses, tame,
> Lifted its perfect head and came
>   To welcome us.

'Midsummer', in its joyful pastoralism, is perhaps the only one
of these poems fully absorbed in the happiness of love.

'Soft to your Places' keeps time's effects at bay, but 'A
Lady of Quality' is a more complex consideration,
incorporating the memory of past love, its present evanescent
state and questions about its legacy of future memories. The
best lines come towards the beginning where the details of
the hospital are distinguished by a stiff lifeless quality; the
aseptic properties of the sick room have a provisional grace,
as do the conventional gifts of books and flowers given 'To
bless the room from present dread/ Just for a brittle while'.

Against this pretence are set images of the greater and
more natural freedoms of the out-of-doors which carries
memories of love's better hours—before the present dread.
One stanza captures the unhappiness of love's termination:

> 'Ended and done with' never ceases,
> Constantly the heart releases
>   Wild geese to the past.
> Look, how they circle poignant places,
> Falling to sorrow's fowling pieces
>   With soft plumage aghast.

The speaker's attitude to the present is beautifully reflected

21

here in the echoing refrain-like 'Ended and done with', in the image of the heart exiled from love like a flock homing to places once secure and familiar and being shot down by sorrow personified as a hunter. There is an echo here of Irish exiles after the Siege of Limerick in 1691, the original Wild Geese of Irish history. Even the archaism of 'fowling-pieces' blends with the historical reference, and the ambiguity of 'fowl' and 'foul' is effective.

The poem moves thereafter to a firm and logical acceptance of love's interruption, as the speaker looks for an alternative, something to set against time's eroding action. The change of tone is modified by the emotional context of his choice: regret at its necessity, recognition that it is less than ideal and tenderness for the pain caused to his beloved. The 'qualities' that remain have to do with persistence; their justification involves showing them to be of some human worth.

In these love poems the beloved is individualized, but in those that belong to the second kind of poem she is more the Muse of poetry, the source of inspiration, than any actual person. They are not so much personal responses to other human beings or human situations as compulsive orchestrations of images. To some extent they are the most original poems in the book, less imitative in manner and more in keeping with Kinsella's need for orderly relationships. That need finds satisfaction in bringing a complex of themes into parallel and mutually illuminating alignment ('Ulysses'), in a dramatic, dream-like meditation on the self and its relationship to cosmic and geological perspectives ('An Ancient Ballet'), or in joining the biological self to the temporal motions that affect all that is ('Who Is My Proper Art').

Of the three, 'Ulysses' is the most successful, mainly because it handles the language better to create a vivid and richly suggestive mingling of its three thematic layers. Its complex pattern is developed on the similarities between Ulysses striving for Ithaca after the destruction of Troy, the year searching for spring after autumn, and a lover yearning

for a fully-satisfying relationship. Each thematic layer is an
analogy for the others. The 'smashed trellis' of summer
vegetation serves as a metaphor for the destruction of Troy.
The 'Tale' is the story of the Trojan War, the 'polis' is Troy
itself. Ulysses undergoing his ten-year journey back to
Penelope—'Eden locked still in Odysseus'—is like the seed
underground in winter and like any man waiting for love. The
various failings of Odysseus, the year and lovers are a
necessary part of progress towards fulfilment: persistence
through disappointment, change and loss eventually brings
success.

Many poems in *Another September* express a general sense
of threat which shadows even the love lyrics. In this third
kind of poem, the nature of the threat is not made fully
clear. The poems convey a sense of loss which is not so much
their theme as the condition from which they emerge. The
prophetic speaker in 'Lent Is For Repentance' calls attention
to the presence of sickness, tiredness and death. 'Clarence
Mangan' speaks of a blight on human activity and of
unhappiness and terror. 'The Monk' takes delight in death to
which 'Pause en Route' speaks directly, but glibly. The
bride-companion of 'In the Ringwood' is transformed to
'Sorrow's daughter' and in this poem love is recurrently
broken; all things are subject to 'Dread, a grey devourer,/
Stalks in the shade of love'. 'The Fifth Season' asserts a
philosophical acceptance of these general characteristics: loss,
pain, death sharpen one's appreciation of present values. The
first stanza of 'An Outdoor Gallery' defines Kinsella's
prevailing outlook at this stage of his career:

> Life was a mute wrenching of the heart,
> A wound in the red roof of the mouth. Often
> The very accomplishment of its bitterness
> Insisted one should smile and, smiling, accept.

The effects of such a threatening context of living are visible
in various ways in these poems. What we find is a cold, even
distasteful recognition and discovery of a world that is

painful to the senses, the intellect and the imagination, but the development in the book is towards a deeper perception of life's darker forces and to a firmer understanding of the place of the artist. Kinsella is here a meditative poet in the making. We begin to see his distinctive and defining artistic vision, even as he himself comes to see, painfully, obscurely and doggedly, what being an artist means in his case. For him the essential fact is that he lives in a world constantly undergoing the processes of decay and that the forces controlling decay are immediate, violent and compelling.

The idea of confrontation may be seen in the opening lines of 'Baggot Street Deserta', which is a tentative statement, at an early stage, of Kinsella's views on the role of the artist and a definition of the factors that count in his universe. (He will make the statement again in a more complete way that includes the love relationship, and in the same setting, at the end of 'Phoenix Park'.) The poem begins after a period of artistic endeavour which is described, significantly, as an 'attack', an operation of the will in a situation that is tortuous—'The breaking-cry, the strain of the rack'. The making of poetry is seen as something aggressive, a possession of the artist, a force to which he has to yield.

The poem proceeds in a mood of recovered calm, in the 'silence' and 'peace' that follow the strenuous engagement of the artist with his material. The abrupt, disrupted rhythm of the lines also yields to a longer, more even-flowing sequence in which the speaker turns his attention to larger horizons. From the initial view of the isolated, tortured individual, we have an inclusive meditative focussing of stars, music, the river and Dubliners. The relationship between the individual and this lyric scenario begins as a blunt contrast but is gradually refined in the course of the poem into a harmony expressed in the ample musical rhythm which finally emerges from the broken dissonance of the opening. The sleeping Dubliners are joined to stars, music and river as part of a fundamental rhythm, their heads 'flashing with images'. That objective survey relates the speaker to Kinsella's customary universe of space and time, ever-present change and the human inclination to communicate through images. Within the calm there is flux: the ordered wheeling of the stars, the burdened river searching for the ocean, the rhythmical precision of music and the flickering images of the dreamers.

Section two returns to the speaker and the drab, ordinary context of his life. The mood is disconsolate; identifying with 'A curlew's lingering threadbare cry/ Of common loss', he appropriates the bird as a symbol for his confusion and uncertainty. The challenge for both is 'the spurious'.

> Versing, like an exile, makes
> A virtuoso of the heart,
> Interpreting the old mistakes
> And discords in a work of Art
> For the One, a private masterpiece
> Of doctored recollections.

Out of loss, disunity and error and through re-examination of past experience the artist creates his work.

The hazards are set forth in the imagery of confusion, hallucination, body-snatching, disappointment and nightmarish perversion:

> Looking backward, all is lost;
> The Past becomes a fairy bog
> Alive with fancies, double crossed
> By pad of owl and hoot of dog,
> Where shaven, serious-minded men
> Appear with lucid theses, after
> Which they don the mists again
> With trackless, cotton-silly laughter;
> Secretly a swollen Burke
> Assists a decomposing Hare
> To cart a body of good work
> With midnight mutterings off somewhere;
> The goddess who had light for thighs
> Grows feet of dung and takes to bed,
> Affronting horror-stricken eyes,
> The marsh-bird that children dread.

CHAPTER 1

The goddess stands for the Muse, or more generally, the ultimate possibilities to which the artist may aspire. Here, in the final image that combines the scatological, the sexually perverted and the nightmarish, she is monstrously transformed to a terrifying marsh-bird, the heron or curlew whose cry in the night frightens children.

Such risks do not deter him. Faced with a universe of pain, where change, decay and death are palpable, aggressive facts of existence, Kinsella's response is necessarily and self-defensively strenuous—direct, compulsive, willed, like that of a man fighting an opponent he has not sought, but cannot and will not avoid.

> I nonetheless inflict, endure
> Tedium, intracordal hurt,
> The sting of memory's quick, the drear
> Uprooting, burying, prising apart

These jagged lines project an image of stubborn determination and of suffering. References to the breaking cry, the strain of the rack in the opening lines are echoed, but here the action is both active and passive, an inflicting and an enduring. The whole complex activity in which the poet is both victim and torturer, martyr and masochist, nourishes the creative stream, the 'single stream'. 'Impassioned/ Now with obsessed honesty', he spends the alert sleepless hours in pursuit of truth.

In the next section the poem relates the artist directly to its earlier perspectives. In this calm concluding movement, he notes the intimate connection between his own biological self and the world at large. The 'alien/ Garrison' of his inner life—impulses, instincts, unconscious unknown forces—is part of the order of things, an assertion that Kinsella has made less effectively in earlier poems, particularly in 'Priest and Emperor', and a faith that lies at the heart of his work. Adam's morse, the pulse of life, images within the head, reach out to the extreme fringes of the universe. The garrison metaphor is appropriate to the whole drift of his thoughts on the nature of the artist. The poet is a man possessed by exploratory forces that somehow have entered his inner self and that maintain a contact with the main force of life itself. The link is provided by the imagination which is engaged in pushing out the frontiers of understanding. That relationship between his private self and the unknown explains, justifies and satisfies him. His cigarette, tossed casually into the dark deserted street, a final image of such probing activity, signals the end of his reflections and is a gesture of confidence in the appropriateness and necessity of what he is doing.

Two other poems, each concerned with the process of change, come towards the end of the volume: 'King John's Castle' and 'Lead'. The first, describing what remains of the great medieval castle of Hugh de Lacy which is situated on the river Boyne at Trim, County Meath, alternates meditatively between the castle's present ruined condition and its former strength. Kinsella's response to the ruin begins with his sense of the sheer, oppressive nature of the castle which is conveyed by its physical appearance. He stresses the epic force of the ruin, its downward thrust of power and its former brute control of Meath's great province. Within the castle is an engulfing 'spirit', the active force of decay, a hollowness that has absorbed both the material and the human—'Intriguers foundered into the arms of their own monster'. It is because of this inherent power of self-destruction that the castle interests the poet: despite its epic force, its overwhelming power, it contained its own cancer. Capable once of a full range of activity, from 'moderation' to 'massacre', it exists now as a haunting symbol of death and void, an allegory of the way things are. Other observers may, as the fourth stanza admits, interpret the ruin in other ways, from other angles. Kinsella is mesmerized by its lessons of decay, these sermons in stones that reveal the ultimately unknowable, the unreachable heart of the castle's mystery, views opening 'on progressing phases of void'.

'Lead' is also a vision, more dynamically, of time's immense, relentlessly consuming process, seen this time across geological ages. Broken structures of disused forges are associated with mortality, 'as slight/ As flesh', and with natural decay, 'weak as leaves'. In one intense imaginative sweep the poem traverses back to the origin of matter and the creation of the world:

> Flame-breathing Vulcan in a maker's rage
> Smelted and hammered on his smoking ledge
> A bit to bridle Chaos. Hoof by hoof
> The red smith snared and shod. Life reared its roof
> Over the brilliant back.
> Space locked a door. Time set a rock on edge.
> I held a stallion's eyes, a stuff
> That glared so wild its elements went black.

From that initial union of god and matter, life, space and time originated. The dice of lead found in Luttrell's Glen outside Dublin are the remains of time's erosive attack on what the craftsman-God had made. The speaker broods upon successive craftsmen through the ages who re-enacted Vulcan's harnessing of matter into order. That brilliant image of human will, fiercely involved with the world for artistic purposes, also includes the demolition of the makers themselves. The individual worker is himself drawn into the furnace of annihilation and the poem concludes with references to the impassivity of the earth to artistic creation and to those who engage in it.

Another September conveys its drama of destruction in many modes: the elegantly heroic manner of 'Death of a Queen', 'Test Case' and 'The Travelling Companion'; the *poesie pure* of 'Ulysses', 'An Ancient Ballet' and 'Who Is My Proper Art'; the linguistic graces and gentle cadences of the love lyrics; the dense texture of 'King John's Castle' and the vibrant rhythms of 'Lead'. The book's general lightness and exuberance enable us to modify the tone of Kinsella's own sombre observation that the general effect of these poems 'is to make real, in whatever terms, the passing of time, the frightening exposure of all relationships and feeling to erosion' (note 2). The texture of most of these poems is not derived from that sense of frightening exposure. The danger is there, but Kinsella's stance has a confidence and a nonchalance that may appropriately be illustrated by his own admiration, at this time, for the figure of the bull-dancer in *The Odyssey—A Modern Sequel* by Nikos Kazantzakis.

That figure plays a deadly game gracefully, prepared to execute a pleasing escape feat while being charged by the bull, yet doomed some day to make a fatal slip. The emphasis is on the game, on how well it is played, with what panache, with what perfection of technique. It is, Kinsella said, 'a typically artistic view of life, which can both deny and accept and, from the resulting stress, create' (note 3). Behind this image of the bull dancer lies the book's concept of man striving not towards his own perfectibility, but towards the perfectibility of a Nature wholly indifferent to human waste, so that the world itself is the Abyss. His duty in these circumstances is, in Kinsella's words, 'not to despair but to accept: to build on the abyss with joy, even though—or especially because—he is building from nothingness to nothingness' (note 4). The bull dancers of Knossos are presented by Kazantzakis as the pure manifestation of this heroic and playful response in which terror is transformed into an artistic game.

The way to deal with the destructive forces is to become their master; the answer to a world of erosion is a new world verified by the imagination and created with consummate artistry. Poems are both acts of faith in the power of the imagination and strategies for dealing with the bull of experience. Therefore in such lenten times, when fish is ordained, 'let us eat dolphin/ And make articulate wings of idle hands'. Not all the poems in *Another September* have this resilience; there is a growing seriousness of purpose, or of manner, and less enthusiasm for the dazzle of the act. Love poems, as 'Another September' itself indicates, will be replaced by more moral considerations.

In *Downstream* Kinsella takes up some of these moral concerns. Eventually, these lead to a more inward-looking kind of poetry. The brief engagements in *Another September* are on the whole external in manner, even the personal 'Baggot Street Deserta'; they are products of the rational will. In *Downstream* considerations of man, including artistic man, and his environment, raised into questions about the very nature and power of existence, require more extended treatment and move from man considered in an objective manner to an interest in the psychological and subconscious. Long poems create problems of organization and structure, questions not so pressing in *Another September*, but once the poet attempts to descend into unknown areas of the psyche, questions of language and style also become important. In a general way it may be said that any poet, with the example of *The Waste Land* in front of him and the contemporary confessional mode all about him, must consider to what extent subjective and introspective poetry may be consciously directed and to what extent the unconscious processes should be given scope. Allied with this is the modern view that the form of a work results from the demands and rhythms of personal vision. Looking ahead to *Downstream* and beyond we can see the results of these pressures and ideas on Kinsella's work.

CHAPTER 2

DOWNSTREAM (1962)

Of this second collection one could say that whereas *Another September* reflects the situation, *Downstream* deals with it, for it is in this collection, particularly in the longer poems, that Kinsella develops ways of feeling and seeing to cope with his constrained universe. The book begins with an idealized portrait of domestic fulfilment, but examines thereafter the destructive aspects of the world, as the poet finds his own vocabulary and appropriate symbols for encompassing the aggressive elements of his inner and outer worlds. Significantly, in his poems about journeys into darkness, his explorations of violence, decay and death, he affirms the creative imagination's ability to survive.

'The Laundress', an idealized portrait of domestic peace, celebrates individual fulfilment in a life so lived that the woman and her work are happily integrated. Seated in the sunlit doorway, she is unconsciously joined with fundamental rhythms of the natural world. The poem's chief effect is of movement in calm: a still landscape, poplars 'sharing' the wind, 'dreamed' and 'soared' in a summer trance. The expression of summer's brooding reaches fulfilment in the third stanza where the maturing processes of nature are related to the Laundress' pregnancy. Here, at the climax of the poem, the signals of fish sinking, heels fluttering, heart straining and grain ripening, are mirror images for each other.

> As a fish disturbs the pond
> And sinks without a stain
> The heels of ripeness fluttered

Under her apron. Then
Her heart grew strained and light
As the shell that shields the grain.

The poem creates a harmonious relationship between the woman and nature, sun and field, wind and trees, harvesting and pregnancy, the rich movement to fullness in nature and in man.

By its position at the beginning of the book, 'The Laundress' emphasizes values of domesticity and of harmonious oneness with nature that are denied most other figures in the book, although 'Dick King', another uncritical custodian of positive human value, in his own way is also at one with the universe. Usually the fictive speaker is either a traveller in a fearsome universe or an artist struggling to counter life's aggressions with creative work. Innocent of such attitudes, the Laundress stares 'bluntly' at nature's seasonal round, reading therein no lessons of human or natural decay.

That acceptance of the natural processes is viewed from a different angle in 'Cover Her Face' which confronts an issue that lies at the heart of Kinsella's formative vision—the ultimate failure of the individual in death. The central mystery lies in the unanswered question: 'who understands/ The sheet pulled white and Maura's locked blue hands?' At the heart of things, as he has already noted in 'King John's Castle' and in 'Lead' is a destructive force that consumes the human and the material alike. His concern here too is for man's inability to halt or lessen the impact of death, but the stance is far removed from the superhuman calm of the bull dancer.

Much of the material is deeply painful: the diagrammatic isolation of the figures, the obliteration of the girl's distinctive physical features, the blunt assertions of death's hungering victory. Certain images exert themselves upon our sympathies: the utter incomprehension of the family, so self-effacing, so miserably soaked, so wretched that 'words forsake/Even their comforters'. Reality for them is a formula—'The black official giving discipline/ To shapeless sorrow'. The 'grace of breath' joins them more to him than to their daughter. Lines about her journey through life hold the pity of her premature death that has put a barrier between her and her own flesh and blood. For them she is a strange 'grave derelict', a phrase that captures her 'frown' in death and her abandonment to the earth. Lines that mention 'her few glories' and 'gossamers' contain Kinsella's loyalties to human, particularly female fragility:

> Her slightness, the fine metal of her hair spread out,
> Her cracked, sweet laugh.

The poet casts a cold eye on death but not on those afflicted by it; his submission to it is without consolation, but his sight of it is lucid and shared by the inconsolable family. In sharing the blunt experience of death, the poet counteracts the bluntness, for to feel inconsolable in company has some consoling aspects. The occasion of the poem is suffused with feeling, not with articulate grief, but with the numbness or dullness of the family and the observer under the shock of the event. That faithfulness affects the tone, the matter and the language of the poem and marks a significant stage in Kinsella's approach. Central to the whole scene is the stricken speaker, almost 'doodling' with his analysis of what he sees and what it means: 'I cannot deny her death, protest, nor grieve'. It is his total acceptance that is important, that moulds his response, that determines the material and the manner of the poem. His noting of the tawdriness of grief's surroundings is one example of this—the 'drab walls', the faded and peeling wallpaper; these are being accepted in the poem along with the death, the grief and the observer's state of mind. The result is that by refusing to be a conventional elegy, by refusing to elevate the occasion or to distort it by consolation, the poem compels our understanding of the actuality of death and its effects. The 'peace' mentioned, although echoed from James 3:18, is not the conventional, Christian R.I.P., but resembles the state found in 'The

Laundress' or 'Dick King' which arises from the identification with natural processes. As in the case of Dick King, it is not necessarily happiness, but the continuum in which love may try to persist, or in which 'justice' may actually exist. Acceptance, so rendered, may lead to understanding. 'There, newly trembling, others grope for function.'

'Cover Her Face' and 'The Laundress' may be taken as related and contrasting poems expressing Kinsella's idea of acceptance. 'Old Harry' also makes a distinction in its prologue between the harmonious death of the innocent and the retributive end of the guilty. 'A Portrait of the Engineer' similarly brings two types of creative figures together, each a victim of his own particular drive. The Engineer's 'dour intensity' that compels him to build 'Monuments to storm and stress' is the legacy handed on to his successors, whose human function it is to be possessed by the same 'demon'. Since the artist is also possessed by one of 'the brutal arts', his analysis of the Engineer's work and legacy leads him to accept the other's drive which he hates, admires, and understands.

> O should it come
> To pass at length that our ghosts met,
> We'd match our hatreds in a gaze:
> Mine for the flesh his engines ate,
> His for the blurred response of a phrase.

The condemnation of the Engineer, one driven to 'pester/ The lazy places of the earth' is of a person opposite in quality to the Laundress who is so totally in tune with nature. All the poems in *Downstream* show evidence of that moral concern predicted in 'Another September'. It is an integral part of 'Moralities', a sequence of epigrammatic poems in Section II on the topics Faith, Love, Death and Song, and to a lesser degree is to be found in Section IV where the lyrics, more personal and subjective in scope, anticipate later directions in Kinsella's work. It lies at the heart of the three long poems—'Old Harry', 'A Country Walk' and 'Downstream' n Section III.

The long poems were written more or less together and in ɛach 'the single idea which gave rise to the poem developed ... nto generalisations and allegory' (note 1). Generalizations and allegory, that is, about similar concerns—human evil, its effects on individual lives, on the human consciousness and the imagination, and how the individual might hope to survive in the face of the nightmarish evidence of that evil and the sense of the precariousness of life itself that it thrusts before our eyes. Kjnsella's imagination is concentrated by these issues; his technical problem is to project this vision of inherent and inescapable evil and to convey at the same time his sense of those orderly and acceptable relationships which he detected.

'Old Harry' relies on the depiction of the evil personality within a defining and illuminating context. In Eliot's distinctions, it is a poem in the third voice. Furthermore, it is written to illustrate a specific thesis and the element of conscious direction is strong. 'A Country Walk', a descriptive poem with a figure within a defining landscape of place and time, works through the responses created in the walker by his encounter with, by the engagement of his consciousness by, details of a particular place with a particular history. Because the surroundings are granted a naturalistic authenticity and autonomy, independent of the walker, they affect him the more strongly. The drama of psychological change in this case is a development within the figure, whereas in 'Old Harry' the drama is restricted to the contrast between past and present and directed towards a full picture of the character. In the second poem the treatment is at once more detailed and more precise and, indeed, more serious, whereas 'Old Harry' is marred by its rhetorical virtuosity. 'A Country Walk' provides a carefully disciplined and controlled revelation of the interaction of person and environment. Towards the end, to demonstrate the effects of Irish society upon him, the manner shifts from the objective to the subjective. Here, the poem moves closer to being of the first voice; it is the texture of the lines that conveys aspects of the walker's subconscious. Its coherence depends more on the consistency of feeling than on the sequence of events, objects and ideas that determined the poem's growth in the earlier sections. That change in method anticipates 'Nightwalker' which, almost entirely introspective, depends for its structure on the fluid associations of images surfacing in the walker's consciousness. In that later poem external data derive whatever significance they have from their part in the internal life of the walker. 'Downstream' lies close to 'Old Harry' in its luxuriance of language, although this was effectively pruned in subsequent versions, but it also anticipates 'Nightwalker' in that the connection between the traveller and the terrain is more intimate than in 'A Country Walk'. Instead of the alert and distinctive personality found in 'A Country Walk', we have an almost mystical communication and identification with the natural scene. Those aspects of mystery and suggested evil sensed by the speaker on his way to the holy city of Durrow reinforce his subconscious sense of evil and death. They revive and confirm what he has already felt. In both 'A Country Walk' and 'Downstream', as Kinsella has observed, 'events so arrange themselves as to impose on the traveller an emotional acceptance of the reality of death, and the beginning of a possible understanding' (note 2). The 'process of increasing awareness' in these two poems is necessarily absent from 'Old Harry' whose consciousness is dead to the signatures of the natural world.

'Old Harry' is a psychological drama in five sections, with a prologue in which Death states the theme of death and retribution and in which the speaker 'in pity' sees 'Body and spirit.../ Drink up their sour ordeal, heaped with curses', and a 'Vale' that restates the distinction made in the prologue between the harmonious, not necessarily painless end of the innocent and the retributive, not necessarily painful end of the guilty. The five main sections entitled 'The Twilight of Old Harry' are not chronological: numbers i, iv and v take place after ii and iii which are part of Old Harry's memory as he leans against the tree in section i.

Section i introduces Old Harry: a 'crumpled lion' whose

death-like progress through the fecund wood terrifies its
creatures. Oppositions between his broken figure and the
vital surroundings serve to define him and lead to the
concluding contrast: 'He laid on the rich red tree his mottled
hand'.

That death-like touch is part of his blindness and insen-
sitivity, the aspects of his character that sections ii and iii will
develop. In section v, sunk deeply into his private 'dream', he
fails to understand the falling leaf's retributive touch, even
forgetting at that stage his memories of atomic horrors from
section iii. The poem's method is that of dramatic contrasts
between the sections, of which the major contrast is between
these frame-sections i and v and the two intervening,
revelatory sections iii and iv. The man's moral failure is
emphasized in section v, when he is moved not by abhorrence
of what he has done but, repulsively, to a 'vacant memory of
mucous pleasure', and, shockingly, to his 'favourite/martial
music', to which he goes homeward for his tea, whistling.

That failure in understanding and self-criticism is characteristic. In section ii he complacently and nostalgically
reflects on the days and events that led up to his decision to
make use of atomic bombs. His main memories are of
externals—the gleaming table ('his'), 'war organisms', his
'senior and neat' advisers, his own 'bluff final words', the
'smooth globe'. This egotistic projection of himself as the
central figure in the drama is intensified in the second half of
the section where the inflated rhetoric betrays that self-
indulgence. The poem balances the exposure of his day-
dream—'O those fearful days', 'the world spun round/To gusts
of pain', 'trod paths of fury',—and the actuality which the
words also convey. Old Harry is part madman, part Jove, a
demonic evangelist, blind to the horror he does in the name
of good—'to the toy Arctic/ And Boreas blew his dreadful
moral blast'. The pity and the terror of the occasion are
contained here: the dread is both the terrifying deed and its
calamitous effect, but it is also a blast in the most literal
sense imaginable. On one side, these enormities; on the other,
the total irresponsibility of the deed's perpetrator and his

37

inability now to feel either the terror or the human
degradation of his deed—'he inclined/ Rounded cheeks, eyes
like coins'. The tone of these tercets is also binary:
condemning the man's failure to see clearly what he has
done, and sympathizing with his lonely struggle to do what
he thought was right.

Section iii brilliantly recreates the nightmarish consequences of Old Harry's decision, and rises to a surrealistic
climax through images of fire and erotic transformations. His
notion of himself as an instrument of divine retribution,
already visible in the smug justification of 'The greater terror
for the lesser number', is continued in the allusions to the
destruction of Sodom and Gomorrah, which remind us
powerfully that this holocaust is neither divine nor moral. We
are appalled by the fundamental dishonesty of such phrases
as 'notorious cities', 'lascivious streets' and 'melted shyly'.
Playing initially with the notion of wrathful annihilation to
express Old Harry's insane memory and to create the horror,
the section proceeds by orgiastic indulgence of the depraved
imagination through erotic and theatrical scenes.

> Then the notorious cities of the plain,
> Groves of the temporal, lost their flesh and blood,
> Tiles, leaves, wild cries, stripped away by gales of light.
>
> Lascivious streets before they shrivelled up
> Heightened their rouge and welcomed baths of pure flame;
> In broad daylight delicate creatures of love
>
> Swayed in a rose illumination of thighs,
> Their breasts melted shyly and bared the white bone;
> At that sight men blushed fiercely and became shades.

The 'delicate creatures of love' are at once dancers putting on
a show for the delight of men and humans pitifully
undergoing the physical effects of the atomic blast, at one
level strip-tease girls, at another victims of violence. The men
too are at one level observers shamed by the sight of such

degradation, at another victims of the fiery transformation. The erotic undertones are present in the ambivalent meanings: the delighted shock as well as the objective intensity of 'broad daylight'; the sensual and the compassionate in 'delicate'; the mouth-savouring leer and the tender euphemism of 'creatures of love'.

The scene becomes even more grossly and explicitly theatrical as the poem moves from the erotic to the gigantic. The consequences of mankind's release of unimaginable violence is the expulsion of myth and fantasy.

> Anthropophagi moaned in the buckling cloud,
> Amazons and chimaerae, leaving the world.

Anthropophagi, amazons and chimaerae are at one level the distorted creatures of earth, but at another the traumatic effects of such evil on the poetic imagination. Deprived of traditional sources of imaginative nourishment, the contemporary mind is left with Kinsella's blind, inarticulate, barren universe:

> An eye socket with nerves and ducts smouldering,
> A mouth with torn uvula and with no tongue,
> Moistened like two wells the plain's enamelled face.

Section iii has been an orgy of visual imagery, but the result in realistic terms is a reduction of man's capacity for imaginative freedom. Old Harry's hysterical imagination is in itself indicative of those consequences, in particular the failure of the moral sense and of the intelligence.

Section iv deals with the drastic reduction of emotion, gesture and language that followed. In place of the brilliance of section iii, darkness and underground 'twittering', in place of the erotic and theatrical, a terrified constriction in the animal state; instead of people, animals; in place of the natural fecundity and myriad life of section i, barrenness and twitching rats. The partly-humanized beasts represent the degrading release of animality in human nature.

Section v picks up the associations of darkness, silence and winter, but Old Harry remains blind to the enormity of his deed. His scratching connects him with the 'flesh-severing embraces' of iv, his 'mucous pleasure' with the sensuality of iii, the 'martial music' with the 'war organisms' of ii. He shivers, but, lost in 'golden light'—autumn's burnished colours in the wood, the red burnings of iii and his memories of himself 'many golden years ago',—is only dimly and imperfectly aware of winter's touch. Old Harry's moral blindness is conveyed, in part, by his inability to respond to nature.

'A Country Walk' on the other hand is the story of the individual responding to the particulars of the environment, taking in not just the immediate objects of town and countryside, but the influences from the mythical and historical past of the locality and his own personal past. Journeying through a multi-layered world the walker allows its details to shape into meaning and focuses the self through the objects perceived or imagined and the manner of those perceptions. At the poem's highest point, where road and river intersect, he achieves a total awareness of the self in its physical and metaphysical surroundings (note 3).

The whole poem is a lesson of persistence through change. The town itself, its mythology and history, and finally the walker himself, are figures in a large design where the basic pattern is of endurance through time and event.

> Mated, like a fall of rock, with time,
> The place endured its burden: as a froth
> Locked in a swirl of turbulence, a shape
> That forms and fructifies and dies, a wisp
> That hugs the bridge, an omphalos of scraps.

The town has survived time's ruinous processes and its present image in the walker's mind is of 'delicate rigor', 'potent calm', opposites that fuse: an aqueduct ruined but rooted, an asylum both calm and potent. The physical aspects form a metaphor for the walker himself who has just

experienced strain and opposition and here discovers calm
within tension: 'Ferocity became intensity'.

The poem's next stage recalls the town's burden of myth
and history. The 'speckled ford' reminds him of Irish saga—'I
shuddered with a visual sweet excitement'—and he associates
it with a tale combining elements from the fight of Cuchulain
and Ferdia in the Old Irish epic, *The Cattle Raid of Cooley*,
and from the story of Conchobar MacNessa's dying on the
day Christ was crucified. The historical imagination re-
vitalizes the decaying urban scene as the poem moves
chronologically through a further series of violent occur-
rences: the Norman massacre, the Cromwellian butchery, the
Rising of 1798, the bleak nineteenth-century aftermath, the
Rising of 1916, the Anglo-Irish War, the Civil War, and the
depreciation of values in the 'gombeen jungle' of post-
revolutionary Ireland.

Contemporary Ireland is materialistic, a land of shop-
keepers, as Kinsella succinctly says in a listing of names
sanctified by Yeats:

> Around the corner, in an open square,
> I came upon the sombre monuments
> That bear their names: MacDonagh & McBride,
> Merchants; Connolly's Commercial Arms... .

From heroic combat, through idealistic rebellion, through
suffering, to contemporary greed and hypocrisy; the journey
is downward. Appropriately the poem now refers to 'otherworldly gloom' and a downward progress. At the lowermost
point of this descent a drop of moisture, recalling the holy
well and its effects earlier in the poem, signals a change for
the better: 'a single/ Word upon my upturned face '. That
there is more reality and vitality in the past than in the
present is shown in that the Christian Brother, although
familiar, is not drawn into the walker's recreative imagination; and in that the car is stripped of reality by the past
significant life of the place. The dusk and naked trees add to
the prevailing design of failure and barrenness. The walker's

persistent vitality amid these shades is shown by the drop of refreshing rain that absolves him from failure. Through the grace of his creative spirit, he too is an enduring and creative force.

In the final section the imagery of renewal increases; the action and vitality of life is beautifully rendered in the rushes and pauses, the changing pattern of moving water, 'Surfaces that gave and swallowed light'. The 'sweet trade' brought by the symbolic star signals the release of feeling and language. Through the successive acts of awareness and intelligence of which the poem is composed the walker has won through to creativity.

'Downstream' is also an archetypal journey into the underworld of death and horror, with its consequent clarification of purpose. The poem begins at dusk, in a ghostly atmosphere, as two travellers move blindly into a strange wooded region where the river channel narrows and suggestions of terror grow. The narrator is particularly susceptible to the atmosphere; for him roots in the river bed 'crawl' to 'cage' them in and 'furred night-brutes' watch from the banks. Sounds in the night stir him to fearful questions.

These premonitions of evil awaken memories of a childhood terror associated with these woods where a man sickened and died, his 'shell' left half-eaten to 'frighten stumbling children'. It was a time of general violence, with Europe undergoing the destructions of the Second World War and Ireland watching, burdened by her own 700 years' heritage of war and oppression. For the boy the time was nightmarish; by day the 'barren world' lit by the conflagration caused by 'swinish men', by night, hellish dreams of human animality,

> the evil dream where rodents ply,
> Man-rumped, sow-headed, busy with whip and maul

> Among nude herds of the damned.

The joint experience of the death in the woods and the war

was traumatic, an irrevocable disruption of youth's innocent notions of death as something formal, peaceful and picturesque.

The final stage of the journey brings them to the heart of the mystery: an ambiguous blend of good and evil, white and black, bird and beast. Beneath the horror lies a complex pattern discernible to the adult. These discoveries of an understandable order are suggested first in the corpse's calm encounter with the stars, but they are given stronger emphasis in the deep fathoms of the Mill-Hole, when the river bed calls to their flesh. Images of good and evil, white and dark, swan and snake, Christ and Judas gather in the darkness: 'A shuffle of wings betrayed with a feathery kiss/ A soul of white with darkness for a nest'. Lifting his eyes to the heavens, the narrator has a vision of cosmic order and of a pattern in life and death.

> The phantoms of the overhanging sky
>   Occupied their stations and descended;
>   Another moment, to the starlit eye,
>
> The slow, downstreaming dead, it seemed, were blended
>   One with those silver hordes and briefly shared
>   Their order, glittering.

In this momentary sensing of order, he and all the living are carried forward through successive encounters with evil behind which lurks the grace of a universal design. But that vision of the harmonious relationships is brief and illusory. The reality at the end of the journey is a 'barrier of rock' that blots heaven from the view. The confrontation is between the speaker and that rock in the dark, with its 'varied barrenness'. 'Downstream' carried the traveller further than either of the other two long poems. The added dimension gained on this journey is an understanding of a balance in nature, a maturer recognition of the fusion of good and evil. The poem provides a resolution to the horrors conveyed in all three poems and a reason for acceptance in its final momentary and confirming vision of a universal pattern. The ultimate vision in these poems is found not in monastic Durrow with its saintly dead, nor indeed in boyish innocence, but in clear though momentary recognitions of a cosmic order.

It may be noted here that the Second World War was traumatic in its presentation of the ineluctable evidence of evil; a realization that was devastating to the imagination and that forced linguistic restrictions on the poet. The 'varied barrenness' of that 'barrier of rock' remains as a fundamental element in Kinsella's outlook, confronted again and more directly at the end of 'Nightwalker', in a poem in which the war itself is employed as the most comprehensive and strongest evidence of the violence inherent in man, encountered yet again in *Finistère*, and prevailing in much of the starved terrain of *Notes From the Land of the Dead*. The sterile and depressive universe first conveyed in stark detail in *Downstream* is something that Kinsella has to absorb into poetry. Fundamentally, the problem is one of language, or of translating a concept of existence, of endurance, into words, since the quest for order, for love, for moral values amid appalling conditions of action and feeling, necessarily involves the search for a language adequate to the terms of that search and the nature of its motivations.

Kinsella's realization of the need is signalled at the end of *Downstream* in the poem 'Mirror in February'. Here, anticipating the verbal cunning and the human anguish of *Nightwalker*, he equates and combines emotional hurts with linguistic curbs.

> Below my window the awakening trees,
> Hacked clean for better bearing, stand defaced
> Suffering their brute necessities,
> And how should flesh not quail that span for span
> Is mutilated more?

The paradox at the centre of his search for love and understanding is that the most severe lesions of suffering reveal the most illuminating sense of form and value. Out of the deepest and most intense experience of pain comes his clearest revelation of that which makes existence bearable and love and art possible. Poems in *Notes From the Land of the Dead* will say this with radical force, but it is also fundamental to *Nightwalker*, where it is the gift he offers the beloved.

CHAPTER 3

NIGHTWALKER and Other Poems (1968)

The opening poem, 'Our Mother', has a similar setting to 'A Lady of Quality' but the gorgon figures in this hospital, three women at different stages of life's contribution of pain, suffering, compassion and death, are brought together as isolated images of a common experience. Between them they determine the speaker's life: 'Living, dying, I meet their stare/ Everywhere, and cannot move'. Life is a process of dying, a fact he observes in them, as also in himself: the double application is contained in the ambiguity of 'living, dying', which can refer both to himself and to the women figures. That unity of sympathy and understanding is found in the mother's identification with the daughter in her pain and in the speaker's equally tender view of the mother as herself an emblem of individual suffering. Her union of fragility, persistence and clear-eyed courage is the moral Kinsella steadily develops and finally celebrates throughout the book.

> ... —a revenant
> A rain-worn, delicate
> Stone shape that has looked long
> Into that other face direct.

Even when the theme is less directly personal, as in 'Landscape and Figure', the poetry works through realistic details. The generalizations are conveyed within the concrete and the specific. The bareness of means predicted in 'Mirror in February' results in a more vital loading of meaning into

47

directly presented observations. Kinsella can be both intimate and private, as in 'Our Mother', or objective and theoretical, as in 'Landscape and Figure'. His range of attitude and expression is flexible, less inhibited than heretofore by the difficulties and depressive aspects of his personal view of existence.

'Landscape and Figure' might be taken as a more realistic statement of 'The Laundress' by an alienated sensibility sharply aware of destruction as an inescapable factor of existence. Again the poet accepts that life is a form of death, but with the difference that here he unites the context of human existence with natural forces. Man and landscape are joined by the same tyrannies of 'blight' and 'flower', death and life.

> A man stoops low on the overcast plain. He is earthing
> Or uprooting among heavy leaves. In the whole field
> One dull poppy burns, on the drill by his boots.
>
> The furrows yield to his care. He does not
> Lift his head; and would not, though the blight
> Breathed on his fields out of the low clouds.
>
> The blight breathes, or does not, invisibly,
> As it will. Stalks still break into scattered flower.
> Tissue forms about purpose as about seed.
>
> He works toward the fruit of Adam. It darkens the plain,
> Its seed a huge brain. The protecting flesh
> When it falls will melt away in a kind of mud.

The two complementary themes of life and death pervade and unify the poem. Thus the man is either 'earthing' or 'uprooting', two tasks that express the extremes of activity and contain the ideas of life in the sense of fertility and death in the sense of harvest. That it is impossible to distinguish one activity from the other prepares for the poem's conclusion in which death and life become identified. The context for human activity is here viewed in an elementary relationship of man and earth. His bent posture under the heavy sky describes him. The poppy is an image of life, but its intensity may be not only of colour but of immolation. For the man it is both purpose and opiate, helping to spur him to endeavour, but also helping to dull his sensitivity to the circumstances of his existence. His 'care' is both attention and worry, the 'furrows' may also be both agricultural and lines of care.

This second stanza alleviates the view of man in the first stanza. Although the reward may be slight, his work is not without result. His refusal to raise his head indicates both his determination to pursue his appointed task and his evasion of 'the blight'. The presence of decay, even if aggressive, would not deter him from doing what he is doing, because his victory is in the passivity of furrows. Two freedoms are juxtaposed: the man's freedom to work at what succeeds for him and the blight's freedom to be. In the poem's most poetic third stanza life is affirmed as an active, untamable force.

> Stalks still break into scattered flower.
> Tissue forms about purpose as about seed.

Here lies the justification for human persistence: the activity of the man and the proliferation of nature. 'Purpose' itself is a virtue and its own reward.

In the final stanza the figure is made explicitly representative of human endeavour at any stage on the evolutionary road. The end comes only with the final dissolution of mankind: existence is given value by being placed within a process of fulfilment. Ultimately the blight that hangs over him is that final death. Human dissolution returns man to the earth itself, towards which the figure in the poem has been pushed from the opening line. This is a figurative return to the slime of the earth either by natural processes or by any catastrophe, such as an atomic holocaust, that also reduces man to a 'kind of mud'. Natural put-

CHAPTER 3

rescence is the positive solution; the negative is that melting of flesh described in 'Old Harry'.

There is a creative, synthesizing forward motion that counters, although it does not eradicate, the destructive motion. In 'Museum' Kinsella condemns the curator who does not consider this 'onward turbulence of forms'. In 'Traveller' the artist in a state of doldrums is pulled back to his proper 'predatory' task by the sight of the owl-Muse 'eating'. In 'Westland Row' the artist as dulled commuter is halted by his vision of the girl-Muse as a real person standing against a stream of shadows. The artist, in particular, lives on the brink of existence, at the edge of evolution. Aogán Ó Rathaille in 'The Poet Egan O'Rahilly, Homesick in Old Age', makes poems to nourish the spirit of his abandoned people. Keats in 'To Autumn', himself but a 'phantasm of flesh', elicits a moment's stay against erosion.

> Along ethereal summits,
> A gleam of disintegrating materials
> Held a frail instant at unearthly heights.

The poet is at the edge of consciousness, like the grub in 'Leaf Eater' reaching out 'in blind/ Space' or like the toads in 'Folk Wisdom' terrified by impending doom. The miracle is that out of such intense realization of pain beauty may come:

> As when a man
> Clutches his ears, deafened
> By his world, to find a jewel
> Made of pain in his hands.

References in these lyrics to the groping, predatory nature of things, as also to their synthesizing process, express Kinsella's concept of life and matter. The groping verticil of the grub on the leaf, the blunt probe of the teddy-bear's stare in 'Soft Toy', the imagination's outward thrust and the acceptance of life's anguish are all metaphors for his informing vision of life. The central philosophy of endurance and renewal, expressed in these poems and in the *Wormwood* sequence, is related to the fundamental idea that there is a purposeful direction in an otherwise unbearably anguished world. That there is a common, basic process at work helps to explain these identifications of man and matter.

Nightwalker on the whole is less concerned with general manifestations of nightmarish evil than with immediate experiences of pain. Individual anguish on earth, in marriage, or as an artist caught up in the duties of domestic or professional life expresses Kinsella's personal involvement with immediate problems. The response on the whole is positive: out of life's daily grind may come moments of understanding and through endurance come maturity and peace. Although man is lost in a blighted landscape, he participates in an orderly process of growth leading towards death. On those terms he is granted the possibility of a succession of triumphs in which life's bitterness may be absorbed and transmuted. By confronting an almost overwhelming disaster, he gains a sense of value which, rooted in his personal experience, flowers into a conviction. The force of this conviction is in proportion to the suffering which sponsored it. It is expressed with particular force in the *Wormwood* poems.

The seven *Wormwood* poems, which are related thematically and stylistically to the other lyrics in this collection, describe a marriage relationship that is painful, mutually agonizing, yet ultimately acceptable. Love is the only support the partners have as they clasp 'sighing', 'propped above nothing'. Their union endures even though their nights are racked by dreams that correspond to the hideousness of their lives, and their days are passed in the unblinking awareness that they live in bitterness.

The introductory poem captures the ambiguity of their position:

> Open this and you will see
> A waste, a nearly naked tree
> That will not rest till it is bare,

51

> But shivers, shivers in the air
> Scraping at its yellow leaves.
> Winter, when the tempest heaves,
> It riots in the heaven-sent
> Convulsions of self-punishment.
>
> What cannot rest till it is bare,
> Though branches crack and fibres tear?

The tone of this invitation is objective and confident. The tree in its final stages of stripping exhibits the same dualistic perspectives as those expressed in 'Landscape and Figure'. Its paradoxical state is expressed in the ambiguities of 'riots' and 'heaven-sent', meaning both the tossing of the tree in the storm, an external aggressive force, and the exultation of the tree in destruction which it masochistically regards as beneficent. Its condition is so unbearable that the termination of life is actively sought. Thus natural degeneration is supported by self-inflicted destruction. The concluding riddle refers immediately to the emblematical tree, but that it is posed at all implies other referents, such as the human heart, the couple joined as a single tree, or the book of poems that make up 'Wormwood'. Peace, rest from activity, only come in death; meanwhile, despite the anguish, the tree's nature and by implication the character of the poem and of man is to endure. The tree, ambiguously, both 'will not' and 'cannot' rest.

This introductory poem deals resolutely with its agonized subject. The rhythm of the lines with their four definite stresses and rhyming couplets conveys the strength of the position. Despite the numerous references to shivering, the irony of 'riots' is dominant. 'Wormwood' itself refers to the star of the Apocalypse whose fall to earth changed a third of the waters into a bitterness from which many men died:

> and a great star fell from heaven, burning
> as it were a torch; and it fell on the
> third part of the rivers and upon the fountains

52

> of waters; and the name of the star is
> called Wormwood; and the third part of
> the waters became wormwood; and many men
> died of the waters, because they were made
> bitter.
>
> Apocalypse: Ch. 8, vv. 10 and 11

The poem begins in an awakening from nightmare and renders, as it develops, the speaker's gradual realization of what the nightmare was. The fourth stanza clarifies his dream:

> The two trunks in their infinitesimal dance of growth
> Have turned completely about one another, their join
> A slowly twisted scar, that I recognise... .

The trees are not only interlocking as they grow, they are jointly scarred by their close growth together, an infinitesimal process. They are being slowly destroyed from the outside even as they slowly ascend. 'Iron sinks in the gasping core'. These axe strokes are the intermittent catastrophes that bring them to consciousness, and that will go on until they are destroyed.

'Wormwood' introduces the marriage relationship: the nightmare from which the speaker cannot escape has come 'again', but, although the process is recurrent, unavoidable and terrifying, the emphasis is on recurrence and endurance.

> Remember how we have climbed
> The peaks of stress and stood
> Wearily, again
> And again, face to face
> Across the narrow abyss.

Their sexual union is an angry, hideous burning and groping. They are joined, yet isolated as they enact their 'nocturnal/ Suicidal dance '. Of the two the man's state is the more complex, since his world is centred in her and he is despairingly conscious of the 'fuming abyss' that divides them, and of mortality.

In 'First Light' lover and beloved have 'kept/ Another vigil far/ Into the night, and raved and wept.' With the dawn comes the awakening to the 'unendurable' reality of day. The analogy is with a religious occasion, a watching on the eve of a feastday. The implications are thus positive and the sequence of poems moves towards acceptance. 'Remembering Old Wars' recapitulates the marriage relationship as one of decay; their corruptible flesh stinks of waste. With the dawn they labour upright to face adversity. Paradoxically, like lovers, they 'renew each other', but with a 'savage smile'.

> Sighing in one another's
> Iron arms, propped above nothing,
> We praise Love the limiter.

The condensed meanings here reflect the situation in its restraints and acceptances: the 'sighing' is grief for their anguish, but also pain transmuted to love; they lament but they also 'praise'. The 'iron arms' are the prison in which they are clamped together till death, but also the strength the derive from their mutual support. They are 'proppe(as above a deadly void into which they may fall, but they are also 'propped' in the sense of being mutually supported. As long as their love continues they are saved. Faced with the void of death, isolated beyond 'hope of change or peace', they celebrate the love whose negative restrictions they have made positive. Who actually says 'Je t'adore' is not indicated but it applies to both of them. It is a remarkable testimony to the integrity of these poems and of the relationship they express that they can conclude on such a note. That relationship has been described by Kinsella in an introduction to the *Wormwood* poems, although it may readily be applied to other poems in this collection where the ethic of suffering is fundamental.

> Beloved,
> A little of what we have found ...

It is certain that maturity and peace are to be
sought through ordeal after ordeal, and it seems
that the search continues until we fail. We reach
after each new beginning, penetrating our context
to know ourselves, and our knowledge increases until
we recognise again (more profoundly each time) our
pain, indignity and triviality. This bitter cup is
offered, heaped with curses, and we must drink or
die. And even though we drink we may also die, if
every drop of bitterness—that rots the flesh—is
not transmuted. (Certainly the individual plight is
hideous, each torturing each, but we are guilty,
seeing this, to believe that our common plight is
only hideous. Believing this, we make it so: pigs
in a slaughteryard that turn and savage each other
in a common desperation and disorder.) Death,
either way, is guilt and failure. But if we drink
the bitterness and can transmute it and continue,
we resume in candour and doubt the only individual
joy—the restored necessity to learn. Sensing a
wider scope, a more penetrating harmony, we begin
again in a higher innocence to grow toward the next
ordeal.
Love also, it seems, will continue until we fail:
in the sensing of the wider scope, in the growth
toward it, in the swallowing and absorption of
bitterness, in the resumed innocence...

The natural setting for the *Wormwood* poems resembles the
landscape in 'Landscape and Figure' and is a metaphor for
the bitter waters that cause death. In 'Wormwood' the
speaker stands 'among wet trees' where the ground is a
mossy, almost colourless floor that 'disappears/ In depths of
rain among the tree shapes'. Out of this moisture-laden scene
comes his vision of the 'black tree' with 'blurred branches'
and the emblematic tree rises out of the death-dealing waters.
In 'First Light' dawn comes like a pale gas, a poisonous
exhalation overrunning the garden. The grass is soaked with a

CHAPTER 3

'grey dew'. The natural setting is always devoid of colour and vitality: an appropriate and defining world for these lovers.

Only one poem, 'The Secret Garden', considers the natural world in which humanity must endure existence. It too is a vision poem in the sense that the speaker sees into the reality of things. Nature is tough and threatening, suffering from decay and in turn causing destruction. To be adult is to have acquired the taint of decay and to deal with the aggressive environment. In the relationship of father and son, Kinsella dramatizes the beauty, energy and innocence of the child who nevertheless must be set free 'toward the sour encounter' and the wisdom and weariness of the man whose life has purpose. The child's 'immaculate' state is an illusion. The last lines express the father's weariness, his sense of transience, and his certainty that dew becomes dust, that all life funnels harshly into death. His gardening is at best a momentary, minute stay against nature's grasping, insistent, erosive force. In the secret garden lessons of corruptibility abound.

> ... I cultivate my garden for the dew:
>
> A rasping boredom funnels into death!
> The sun climbs, a creature of one day,
> And the dew dries to dust.
> My hand strays out and picks off one sick leaf.

The 'dew' is the poem's image for beauty. 'Tiny worlds, drop by drop, tremble/ On thorns and leaves....' But beauty is fragile and impermanent, its 'glittering' the momentary grace of 'toughened branches' that absorb it. The dew is a nourishment but also 'dries to dust'. The child's innocence is similarly an instant of glittering: his fragile state is rendered in images of light, his energy 'light as light', his flesh is 'pearl'. He runs 'glittering' into the sun, and is gone. In that brief passage his loss of light is conveyed, as indeed of life, since the sun will dry the dew. Paradoxically, the father's concern is to release him into life, to bless him with the curse of endurance. That way lies the only hope—in the 'place' that grows 'difficult', where the 'flails of bramble/ Crawl into the lawn'. The poem's concluding lines, quoted above, define the context of life within which man must run his course: 'I cultivate my garden for the dew.' The purpose and the reward are as in 'Landscape and Figure'. Living is a form of dying; existence and time are both subject to the processes that lead to death. 'My hand strays out and picks off one sick leaf': the action is both automatic and willed, both negative and positive. To purge even one decayed leaf is to affirm one's own life and to halt decay.

The theme of individual endurance and death is also present in 'The Shoals Returning', a long poem in section II, but here calamity is absorbed in a powerful descriptive commemoration of a way of life that is harsh, treacherous and accepted. Man becomes his environment, joined to it in an elemental and instinctive way. The closeness of that identification is conveyed in the interchanging qualities of the animate and inanimate, the human and the marine. The central figure of the poem is first presented 'Against depths of marine light'. His eyes are 'Black points of spray'. He is threatened by the Wave of Tóime which in turn is personified as a snarling, hungering creature. Later, in a seaside pub, those who listen to his song are like marine creatures in a defining world: 'Live eyes/ Shine, each open on its rock.' These humans too are 'tainted/ With cold sea wind'. Their response to his song is a biological reaction, its force matching the sea's hunger:

> squat
> Entities turn in cranial darkness
> In the ravenous element
> At the innermost turn of the shell.

The song that compels their response is a revelation of that destiny that will return them to their proper ending:

CHAPTER 3

> the cry
> That can prepare the spirit
> To turn softly and be eaten
> In the smell of brine and blood.

The physical and spiritual shaping of the humans is finally
seen in the figure of the withered man against the 'black
outcrop' of rock at the end of the poem:

> He turns a shrunken mask
> Of cheekbone and jawbone
> And pursed ancient mouth
> On the sea surface.

His eyes look 'out of tortoise lids' while 'A windswept glitter
of light/ Murmurs toward the land'.

The poem conveys the sea's vast strength and changing
aspects in its own powerful rhythms, sonorous cadences, and
precise use of concrete images. It matches the sea's forces
with the human, human life fiercely joined with the fierce
life of the sea, a primitive battling of man and nature.

> The boats waited at Smerwyck,
> Black-skinned, crook-backed,
> On the grass by the drying boat-slip;
> The rocky knife-sharp shore
> Drained bare: crayfish stared:
> Brutal torso of conger
> Slid through a choked slit—
> Naked savagery
> On which, when the eyes lift,
> An infinite sheen alights,
> A sheet of blinding water
> Pierced by black points of rock.
> By nightfall the bay ran cold
> With the distant returning tide
> Under the wall of Mount Brandon.
> The clefts brimmed in darkness.

NIGHTWALKER

*

In an interview given prior to the appearance of *Downstream*, but published later in *The Poet Speaks* (note 1), Kinsella said that he consciously avoided Catholic subjects or Irish subjects as being limited in themselves. 'I cannot think at the moment of anything except two very short poems in *Moralities*, one of the "Seventeenth Century Landscape near Ballyferriter" and the other of "Sisters", where the references are completely and exclusively Irish and where the actual facts behind the references would certainly be unknown to a non-Irish reader.' The statement also holds true of *Downstream* with the single exception of 'A Country Walk' which is placed in a specific Irish setting, draws from the Irish past, and is both historical and contemporary in scope. 'Downstream' itself has not the same density of implication, although the actual journey, which took place in 1954, has quite specific Irish dimensions.

After 'A Country Walk' not only does the poetry become intensely private and increasingly introspective, but the incidence of Irish material grows. It is understandable that as Kinsella was drawn more and more into personal experience he should also deal more completely with those aspects of his own personality which would find meaning in terms of the Irish contexts. 'The Shoals Returning' is but one result of his experience, briefly referred to in the interview, in the Ballyferriter area of county Kerry to which he was strongly attached. That Irish-speaking region of fishermen, small homesteads and villages gave him contact with remnants of that lost culture which he inherited across a century of silence. *Nightwalker* has many poems of such Irish interest: 'Ballydavid Pier' and 'The Shoals Returning'—both set in the Ballyferriter region—'Magnanimity', 'Ritual of Departure', 'Nightwalker', 'Phoenix Park' and the revised 'Downstream'.

This significant increase continued in later work: in the satirical *Butcher's Dozen* (1972), in the autobiographical material in *Notes From The Land of the Dead* (1972), in *A Selected Life* (1972), an elegy for Seán O Riada, and even in

Finistère (1972), where the oceanic journey leads to the Boyne valley and the spirals of Newgrange. 'Ireland', he said in an interview on Radio Eireann (January 1974), 'is a necessary burden, a place I must keep coming back to, I must keep trying to understand. It gets less and less rewarding, but it becomes more and more necessary'.

'Nightwalker', whose setting is the Sandycove area of Dublin Bay, is a fluid narrative in the manner of parts of *Ulysses*. The tower is not Yeats's Norman tower with its winding ancient stair but the Martello tower of the Telemachus episode in *Ulysses*. By specifically locating his poem under the shadow of Joyce's tower, Kinsella indicates his homing instinct for the artist who accepted the here and the now, the 'filthy modern tide' that Yeats, he felt, had avoided, and for the art that elicits order from experiences, from the 'mud' of everyday conditions, instead of imposing it from above.

>   Clean bricks
> Are made of mud; we need them for our tower.

The seemingly random and artless associations of 'Nightwalker' stem from this artistic attitude. Structurally, the poem is a constellation of separate sections within the light and gravity of the moon which is its dominant force. Its theme—the violence inherent in modern life—is projected through the figure of the walker who alternates between impressionistic apprehension of his immediate surroundings and memories that rise to the surface of his mind. His consciousness, left as exposed as possible to the pressures of its associations, is the most positive force in an apathetic and ultimately helpless human situation; it is the only force that can counter the 'consuming' lunar force that is pervasive and ultimately unavoidable. He accepts whatever comes, because the reward for such acceptance is the ability to recognize and to survive bitterness, for the moment. 'With a little patience', as he observes, one discovers meaning. He therefore serves as a medium in the spiritualistic sense for those images that inflict themselves on the screen of his consciousness, and moves in a trance-like state, at the mercy of the various 'influences' that affect him. The 'hive of his brain' refers to the images accumulating in his head, as well as to the other centres of activity in the poem, such as the suburbia, the offices of the Civil Service and the State itself.

Part I

The walker's only certainty, expressed in the opening line, — 'I only know things seem and are not good' — refers most immediately to the moon's destructive presence, although it anticipates the poem's major contrasts between the surface aspects of Irish life and the reality. The disenchanted figure of the walker is isolated from his fellows because of his desolating certainty that their listlessness and his are caused by the enervating glare of the moon whose destructive birth as it was violently sundered from the earth is about to be re-enacted by its equally shattering 'return'. The cosmic devastation of the moon's wrenching passage outward 'meant little' to him 'then'. Now it makes all the difference, dominating his consciousness:

> There it hangs
> A mask of grey dismay sagging open
> In the depths of torture, moron voiceless moon.
> That dark area, the mark of Cain.

The ultimate unforeseen point of his meditative journey is the moon's surface where he will directly confront, because there it has no protecting atmosphere, the actual stuff of violence, its source, its barrenness, its mindless evil:

> It has a human taste, but sterile, odourless.
> Massed human wills...
> A dust plain flickering...
> I think this is the Sea of Disappointment.

61

Meanwhile he deals with conditions on earth.

He is both sarcastic at the blindness of his suburban neighbours and angry at the gross waste of human potential apparent in their death-like state, as revealed in the associative images of shadows, trance, burial alive, fish-like flickerings on the television screen and embalmers in the city of Necropolis. The people are inert, self-absorbed, massed together and exposed to the moon's destructive force. Nor is the walker free from their condition; he is 'tethered' to them. That sense of oneness runs through the poem: he is a victim of what he describes, as well as its product. The representative 'Foxhunter' figure of Part II is his 'dark brother'; his strictures on the country's once violent leaders, those 'dragon men', partly include his own 'dragon half'. The poem's tonal complexity incorporates distaste for and acceptance of the existential contexts.

Thus in the next section he mimes that aspect of himself that joins with the commuters and broods bitterly on the country's loss of values. The time is specifically the late fifties when Ireland turned from isolationism in order to attract foreign investors. The tone is a sarcastic parody of Civil Service style:

> Is it not right to serve
> Our banks and businesses and government
> As together we develop our community
> On clear principles, without fixed ideas?

Kathleen Ní Houlihan, traditional symbol of Ireland, has become a debased Statue of Liberty, standing at the harbour's mouth making a prostitute's beckoning gesture, her name—'Productive Investment'. Her appeal to the nations of the world is calculating, showy and unselective, a travesty of the words enshrined on the Statue of Liberty:

> Lend me your wealth, your cunning and your drive,
> Your arrogant refuse;
>   let my people serve them

> Bottled fury in our new hotels,
> While native businessmen and managers
> Drift with them, chatting, over to the window
> To show them our growing city, give them a feeling
> Of what is possible; our labour pool,
> The tax concessions to foreign capital,
> How to get a nice estate though German,
> Even collect some of our better young artists.

Hers is the suave voice of a commercial and vulgar society prepared to sell itself to foreign wealth.

The walker's recovery from the 'Morose condemnation' of this passage is a sign of his vitality. He recognizes the impotence of such anger and that the artist must be able to create out of the circumstances that make his world. 'Nightwalker' itself is evidence of his ability to do so.

The 'Spirit-skeletons' that introduce the last section of Part I are the constellations ascending into the sky and the configurations of experience that rise to his consciousness out of his day. They are 'Pale influences'. 'Pale' has been used to describe the inert state of those in suburbia; it is also descriptive of the walker's trance-like condition. The influences are those that directly affect Irish life. They also have an astrological level in the suggestion here of a Faust constellation. The predatory ruthless German twins are specific examples of foreign investors who have responded to the country's invitation. These are 'pale' because deadly in the way that the 'pale' moon is deadly. In one grim association the walker judges them:

> I cannot take
> My eyes from their pallor. A red glare
> Plays on their faces, livid with little splashes
> Of blazing fat. The oven door closes.

He has not forgotten the evils so conveniently ignored by his Government. Life in the Civil Service is seen as a complete 'hive' world, where officials 'Work, or overwork, with mixed

motives/ Or none'. Ministers of State, once ruthless and
unfeeling, inheritors of the violent birth of the nation, are
now 'blind' and 'shuffling', numbed by lack of understanding, yet joined by history to those who have died—
'claimed by pattern still living,/ Linked into constellations
with their dead'.

The poem shifts from this personal note of oneness with
these dying tyrants to the more declamatory tone of an
announcer 'popularising' the 'constellation' for a lay
audience. The fable of the 'Wedding Group' recreates some of
the country's bitterest events from the early days of the
nation's birth. The title refers to a photograph of Kevin
O'Higgins' wedding which took place in 1921. Standing are
Eamon de Valera, Kevin O'Higgins and Rory O'Connor, who
was best man. These are the Fox, Groom and Best Man of the
poem. The lines that follow fill out a story of friendship,
betrayal and bloodshed. The Civil War found O'Higgins on
the pro-Treaty side, faced by de Valera and O'Connor on the
Republican, anti-Treaty side. Rory O'Connor's seizure of the
Four Courts helped to precipitate direct military conflict
between the two sides. During the Civil War O'Connor was
the victim of a reprisal-execution reluctantly approved of by
Kevin O'Higgins as Minister for Home Affairs. In 1927
O'Higgins himself was assassinated on his way to Mass, in a
bungled, amateurish killing that left him to die in great
agony. The poem's interest in these and other historical and
living figures is not literal but metaphorical: the fable's events
support a general portrait of violence in the first decade of
the State's founding. That violence also included the execu-
tion of seventy-seven Republicans, acts attributed to
O'Higgins and Ernest Blythe, Minister for Finance in the Free
State Government, the 'Weasel' of the poem. Blythe is also
referred to in his capacity as Director of the Abbey Theatre,
where his influence was paramount after the death of Yeats,
'the Player King'. 'A tragicomical tale' follows: the Fox (de
Valera), unappreciative of the Abbey Theatre, puts it in the
charge of the Weasel who 'pranced about in blithe panto-
mime'. The references here are to de Valera's subsidy to the

Abbey, his occasional praise for it, and to Blythe's policy of
having Gaelic pantomimes performed on the Abbey stage at
Christmastime.

Part I has juxtaposed these separate panels in an effective
manner. The welcoming of ruthless investors by a Government created out of violence signifies a degradation of
national values. The image of Kathleen Ní Houlihan recalls
memories of the country's more noble aspirations towards
freedom from tyranny and injustice and towards a liberal
democracy. The old dream was that the country might take
her place among the nations of the earth with dignity and
pride; the reality in the fifties is a sell-out to the highest
bidder. And the Abbey Theatre, once famous for the highest
idealism that motivated its founders, has suffered a deteriora-
tion in artistic standards in the Ireland that has emerged; the
'great complex gold horn' is now 'hammered' with a 'stick'.

Part II

With the introduction of the 'new young minister' the tone
becomes eerie and chilling. Like figures from medieval Irish
legend, horse and rider emerge terrifyingly out of the waves
to become a new sign in the Irish zodiac: 'Foxhunter'. The
associations are of things monstrous, mechanical and ruthless.
The walker's encouraging shout, 'Father of Authors!',. ad-
dressed to the Joyce figure, is also a ridiculing salute to the
new Government Minister, 'The sonhusband/Coming in his
power', as he undergoes the difficult ordeal of lifting himself
up through the mockery of the people whom he will find
both docile and subservient. The walker grimly mimes their
behaviour, criticizing them as much for their mockery as for
their servility, and calculates Foxhunter's abilities as a
place-seeker and a perpetuator of the pattern of violence
already seen in the country. The 'gates' opened by the 'Iron
Fausts' refer primarily to estates taken over by German
capitalists on which the old hunts went, but also to the gates
of the financial compact referred to in Part I. That the new
figure is referred to as the walker's Jungian 'Dark brother'

indicates the partial identification of the two as products of Irish life in the same period. The Minister is also the 'Father of Otters' in the sense that he encourages the 'Otterfaced' investors of Part I. At the same time, since he creates and to a great extent represents the Ireland of this period, he is the father of authors in the sense that the Joyce-Kinsella attitude to art makes it necessary to make art even out of this unattractive substance. Significantly, this section is specifically placed under the Martello tower and Joyce's aid is invoked directly—'Watcher in the tower, be with me now'.

The poem moves back in time behind the new reign to the 'faint brutality' of the walker's schooldays. Brother Burke's simplistic reasoning and narrowly nationalistic views are drastically contradicted by the poem's account of the new Minister. The contrast involved between what the teacher says and what the walker has actually experienced causes him to react sharply and bluntly in 'fierce pity' as he holds out his 'scalding soup of memories' to counter the teacher's facile rhetoric:

> Pupils from our schools played their part,
> As you know, in the fight for freedom. And you will be
> called
> In your different ways—to work for the native language,
> To show your love by working for your country.
> Today there are Christian Brothers' boys
> Everywhere in the Government—

The walker reverts to the deceiving simplicities of his schooldays by depicting a conventional grouping of Virgin, snake and flowers. He comments sarcastically on that earlier acceptance:

> Adolescents,
> Celibates, we offer up our vows
> To God and Ireland, in Her name, grateful
> That by our studies here they may not lack
> Civil servants in a state of grace.

The parody of Abbey Theatre verse drama with which Part II concludes further judges the teacher's exhortation to the boys to work for the native language. The reality of modern Irish culture is the breakdown of tradition. In the conversation between the seamew and the walker, the bird is Amhairgin, spirit of the Irish language and Irish nationality. The loss of continuity is indicated by the seamew's inability even to hear the walker; her voice is a lonely cry of lament for that loss, as the walker clearly recognizes:

> a dying language echoes
> Across a century's silence.

In a sad recognition of the final evidence of this 'lost soul', he turns homewards.

That things seem and are not good becomes increasingly apparent. The deceiving simplicities of the Christian Brother and the quasi-nationalistic motives of the State are set against the walker's personal experience. Brother Burke conveys a falsely optimistic and debased view of the Irish language; the reality is the lonely, fading voice of Amhairgin. The Commercial Revival of the First Economic Programme, formulated as valuable for the country, results in the debasement of values. The anguish of the walker is to a great extent intensified by his sense of the gulf between appearance and reality. The commercial reign of the newer politician, the unprincipled sale of the country, the failure of educators to prepare the pupils for contemporary living, the disruption of the national tradition, the lifeless quality of human existence, all these are part of his environment. He is their product. He suffers from a sense of aggression and betrayal and for the denial to himself, and to his generation of a life of fulfilment and purpose. The loss is suffered at many levels—cultural, political, national, moral and personal. And behind this immediate local incidence of the quality of life in Ireland lies the walker's corresponding realization of universal evil.

CHAPTER 3

Part III

The sight of 'Her dear shadow on the blind' moves him to state his belief that

> love is half persistence
> A medium in which, from change to change,
> Understanding may be gathered.

Acknowledging the moon's dominance—'moon of my dismay'—he visualizes her response to this poem as wanly approving. The passage illustrates the poem's general method—its reliance on a configuration of contrasting and related elements and its seemingly artless trust in these elements to form themselves into a meaningful design.

> Scattered notes, scraps of newspapers, photographs,
> Begin to flow unevenly toward the pool
> And gather into a book before her stare.

The poem shifts then to the voice of Queen Victoria, lamenting that it was 'a terrible time'. The time is specifically Ireland since the revolution, but also any time of famine, wars, violence and loss. Flat-footed lines describe the moon/Victoria figure, grieving over the world. When she comes 'to take the waters' in a restorative sense, the result is a renewal of 'patience and trust' and a reiteration of Kinsella's own philosophy of persistence, that there is 'a meaningful drama' in the evolutionary process, reaching

> through the years to unknown goals
> In the consciousness of men, which is very soothing.

That shallow benignity of tone contrasts sharply with the walker's own repeated experience of violence. The reality is the moon's violent 'return', as it begins now to drag the water.

The great moon 'mother'—Victoria, Chaos, Night—is the

walker's control. In a final desperate response to her power, he prays for help:

Hatcher of peoples!
Incline from your darkness into mine!
I stand at the ocean's edge, my head fallen back
Heavy with your control, and oppressed!

This is the most outspoken moment of the poem, a climax of identification with the ocean under the moon's power.

The reward for that prayer is a direct confrontation with the actuality of violence itself when the walker is transported to the barren lunar surface. There 'Hard bluish light beats down, to kill/Any bodily thing'. Life is reduced to insects twitching in the dust. It is a measure of the walker's personal freedom from total despair that he calmly and with urbanity—'I believe I have heard/Of this place'—examines the moon's substance. The poem concludes on a note of realization and judgement: this is indeed the Sea of Disappointment, and it has a human taste. The sterility of this environment separates it marginally from life on earth. Here the walker encounters the ultimate state to which the earth and its inhabitants will come. Meanwhile he has his power of persistence, his ability to experience the worst and to survive.

Essentially he is the figure of the artist, undergoing experience between the outer and the inner darknesses. His is 'A brain in the dark'. 'In the mind darkness tosses'. At one extreme is the 'mad stare' of the moon that has already in a violent act plunged 'upward far into the darkness' where it is now 'about to detach/Its hold on the upper night' and return in violence. Darkness is also the prevailing image for the conditions within the walker's personal and social environment. Images advancing to the surface of his consciousness emerge from darkness and are organized as constellations wheeling under the moon's force. All function within Kinsella's concept of darkness within the self, outside it, in all areas of the unknown that the artistic imagination must explore and try to understand. Here the most destructive kind of darkness and evil is the moon. 'Incline', he prays, 'from your darkness into mine'. In that identification of darknesses, the artist's brain is a positive and creative force.

As well as encountering the mark of Cain on the lunar surface, the poem reaches into his own psychic self, as when he withdraws into the shell of his own self to find memories of school:

> snuggle into the skull.
> Total darkness wanders among my bones.
> Lung-tips flutter. Wavelets lap the shingle.
> From the vest's darkness, smell of my body.

or when the poem sees the brain as loosed to experience:

> Gradually, as my brain
> At a great distance swims in the steady light,
> Scattered notes, scraps of newspapers, photographs,
> Begin to flow unevenly toward the pool
> And gather into a book before her stare.

In other words, the walker speaks of 'my brain' in a detached and separate manner. He is frequently the passive recipient of experience. This strategy of helpless involvement with feelings and events, first seen at the end of 'A Country Walk' becomes even more pronounced in *Notes From the Land of the Dead.*

'Nightwalker' is composed of a series of projections of 'states of feeling' in the main figure. In its allusions, its setting, its use of fable and parody, its mimes, its rhythms and its music it traces the events of one mind-at a particular time and in relation to a particular set of external circumstances. Its direction is inward, to the unknowable areas of the self.

'Phoenix Park' on the other hand belongs to the poetry of reasonable reflection. No other poem contains so much of Kinsella's thought, or so successfully blends the dominant themes of his work. His basic philosophy of order elicited from decrease is expressed through a dramatic, growing revelation of order being discovered in the process of writing; the poem itself illustrates what it takes as one of its basic themes.

It is concerned with the quest for a mode of expression and is its own discovery. Further, this quest has another aspect: it is a quest for a love as well as for a language by which bitterness may be absorbed and innocence restored. Love and language are intimate; the discovery of the first in its fullness sponsors the flexibility of the second.

Section I: Stanzas 1-12

The poem begins with cryptic references to departure, return and change, as the lovers make a last visit to Phoenix Park. These allusions reflect his thoughts and it is he also, as the observer-narrator-persona, who notes her responses, gives us the surrounding pastoral details, and points to the impermanence and brittleness of things. The beloved's start of surprise when a twig falls onto the car draws together these growing images of fragility, making them resemble human frailty. That interruptions may come in human relationships is expressed through her question about why he writes her nothing, no love songs, anymore.

The theme of frailty continues in his memories of a visit to her bedside in St Mary's Hospital, also in Phoenix Park. Her fever then, wasting her body, is related to a more general force 'now that eats everything'. At this point the poem advances 'one positive dream' as something that escapes the attack of that general fever. Hesitatingly, he speculates that the dream *is* something he might offer her, with regrets that 'it is not anything for singing'. Her knowledge of things is totally physical and he feels that his dream too she must know bodily.

Before he presents her with the one positive dream, he gives her 'the preparation' for it. Again the setting is within Phoenix Park. There are four separate vignettes: the first of the narrator as child 'devouring mushrooms straight out of the ground:/Death-pallor in their dry flesh, the taste of death', the second of the narrator, later in life, offering himself to the Pond in a gesture of humility and inadequacy: *'Take me./ I am nothing'*. But at that moment in which he is overcome by his sense of human frailty, moved to it by his earlier sight of himself doomed to decay, he senses a metaphysical lesson that the poem itself will try to express: a texture as intricate as the lines of force in a magnetic field, created by the tension between polar opposites.

A further memory brought forward, by way of preparation, is another moment of understanding, when one night he saw the stars 'Changing places among the naked branches/ —Thoughts drawing into order under night's skull'. That vision of the possibility of order is juxtaposed with a rigorous qualification in the final vignette; the tired, emaciated woman who reaches out to him for human contact, despite the shame of her hunger, weariness and poverty, measures human relationship:

> I studied her and saw shame does not matter,
> Nor kindness when there's no answering hunger
> And passed by; her eyes burned... .

The relationship must be serious and real. Otherwise life, time, general erosion and waste remove the more important values from even the kindest, most loving intention. The humans and their feelings simply do not count. The poem moves at once to the intense, fruitful, sustainable relationship of the two lovers. Their process of passionate response and consummation is at first briefly stated and then the subsequent knowledge that 'Giving without tearing is not possible'. Even there exists the paradoxical principle of opposites being within opposites.

The concluding stanza of Section I, not part of 'the preparation' but another stage in their journey from Phoenix Park, has the lovers passing through the Furry Glen, where Sara, their first child, plucked something out of the ground for them 'to admire', an image of thoughtless innocence, undisturbed by the lessons of change and loss, love and destruction that the lover has been reading for the beloved. A cycle has been completed. Sara, plucking, communed with herself just as the narrator-as-child did on the previous occasion. Both instances express first intimations of mortality.

Section II: Stanzas 13-26

This crucial section states the philosophy upon which the poem is built. Its central subject is 'the dream' which interprets the particular insights of 'the preparation'.

As the section opens, the two figures leave Phoenix Park and go to a bar in Lucan. The context is still one of dampness and 'heavy scenes' and the lovers are characterized as before: she is 'uneasy', he absent-mindedly makes signs on the surface of the bar with his wet glass 'In human regret, but human certainty'. Her anxiety, her more passive, less intellectualized, female nature makes it necessary for him to be aggressive, as indeed his masculine nature warrants. The dream will be a parable, signs for her to read, with him as interpreter and instructor.

For him references to leaving, remembering, departure, the sense of a new beginning, a choice about to be made, are not so disquieting, since he has a grittily stoical response to the turns of fortune's wheel. Life being an ordeal, or rather a series of ordeals, which they have hitherto 'welcomed, sour or sweet', it matters little, really, whether they experience it here or elsewhere. The important thing is the willingness, the readiness to 'take and drink' the ordeal-cup. For him the 'ultimate grotesqueries' will 'have to root in more than this sour present'. Clearly, he is more than ready for a change, but her uneasiness must first be dealt with.

In a simple transition he moves from the reality of the signs he makes with his glass to a contemplation of the ordeal-cup that he now wants her to accept. The dream embodies his vision of the world, his proven sense of how things are, what patterns exist, and how the individual must respond to them in order to survive. The mode is metaphysical, embracing life and death, death in life, and the successive victories over the mutable and the mortal that the individual must achieve, if he is to be alive in life, and until the final darkness of death.

Within the cup are signs of order: mirror images of resemblances and correspondences:

> Figure echoes
> Figure faintly in the saturated depths;
>
> Revealed by faint flash of each other
> They light the whole confines....

At this point the lover refers back to the figures from 'the preparation' as supporting evidence for his affirmation that within the bitterness of existence lies a harmonious pattern: the child who plucked death out of the ground was watched by his future adult self, 'a shade'. That shade 'made flesh', who offered himself to the cosmos in a realization of human littleness, 'Stumbles on understanding', even as he begins to fade, just as the child faded, and as he fades he gives way to the daughter in her 'Communion finery'. These succinct, references draw together the stages of life, physical relationships, and process of growing understanding of life and, finally, the recurrent mode by which each individual has to undergo the cycle of birth-growth-generation-and-death for himself. The woman of Section I, the woman who reaches out in the park, the 'you' in the hospital, are more self-contained than the persona, who regards them as 'full of knowledge', the source of his awareness. 'Equipped to learn' by his encounter with the first woman, he then found the beloved in the hospital. The rest of Section II is an intense communication of that knowledge, an intellectual exercise, made in a tone of insistence, but also in a manner that acknowledges the centrality of the beloved both to his discovery of order and to whatever possibility there may be of his continuing to realize order within life's pond of bitterness. Those laws are 'of failure and increase', the ability of the human spirit to recover from the blows of fortune. His belief is that the essence of life is hunger, hunger for order, and that there is no point of completion or satiation within life. Defeat or failure can be adjusted to. The regrouping activity of the crystal continues and even finds new strength in a difficult challenge. These processes of renewal, however, rest on 'the positive dream', on 'undying love'. At this point the tone softens, as he more intimately affirms the essential requirement for his phoenix-like renewals. His final point is that, as long as the positive dream continues the individual spirit exists on the brink of living, reaching out on the edge of consciousness into the 'void', until everything that can be experienced has been assimilated. The metaphor running through these stanzas is life taken as a body, a substance to be eaten, accepted, made part of the flesh, a nourishment demanded by the human being's constant hunger. Life is consumed and the process brings the cup to fulfilment: 'this live world is emptied of its hunger/ While the crystal world, undying, crowds with light/ Filling the cup'.

Finally, he speaks of the 'one last phantasm' presented here as a devouring figure seeking to possess the full crystal, but always unable to accomplish his purpose. He is the final unassimilated potentiality without which hunger (which is life) must cease. Because of this he cannot be assimilated in any terms the human being can understand. He is doomed to pause forever, 'the final kiss ungiveable'. To assimilate this lewd creature is to exhaust this world and to enter the unknown.

Life, the poem concludes, is necessarily destructive and to live it fully is to be afflicted fully by its destructive aspects.

Giving without tearing

Is not possible; to give totality
Is to be torn totally, a nothingness
Reaching out in stasis a pure nothingness.
—Therefore everlasting life, the unmoving
Stare of full desire. Given undying love...

These lines that conclude 'the dream' re-assert *Wormwood's* preface and the philosophy presented here in Section II. The cup of experience absorbs bitterness and in doing so fills to the brim with a succession of victories. At the height of the spiral is the ideal of absolute acceptance of whatever grotesqueries may come, an acceptance based on the confident knowledge that a harmonious transcendence is always possible, all of which rest on the necessary certainty of 'undying love'. The poem reaches a mystical climax in these lines, its rarefied intellectual vision of final calm not easily reduced to literal statements. In the concluding stanza of this section the lover returns his images to her, his mental fever—'mere idea'—to match her body's fever, her physically proven sense of mortality which encourages her to persist in love.

Section III: Stanzas 27-34

Action returns now after the meditational stillness of the preceding section: they drain their glasses in what seems to be a gesture of acceptance of the dream's symbolic cup, 'finish and rise to go'. These gestures help to propel the poem into a different mood in which one hears a note of resumption and of expectation. The lovers return 'again' into the 'saturated air' of the dying season in which he records a fragile image of the beloved:

> You wait a minute on the path, absently
> —Against massed brown trees—tying a flimsy scarf
> At your neck. Fair Ellinor. O Christ thee save.

The apostrophe, taken from 'The Ballad of Lord Thomas and Fair Ellinor' in Percy's *Reliques,* III, 1, is beautifully poignant, reminding him and us of the delicate quality of the subject to whom he has been offering his sour ordeal, reminding us also of the emotional force that she embodies for him. Such fragility of substance resembles the tender fabric of people and things; they too are subject to the axe of circumstances. Seeing her thus outlined against autumn's colours, he has a vivid sensory awareness of the metaphysical structure of Section II. In particular, the 'ghost of that ghost persists', that is, the sense of his metaphysical diagram, but especially the last phantasm trying to get into being, 'insinuating itself into being'.

Such fierce, hungering forces threaten the beloved, the physically weaker partner, but yet the essential one. Seeing her 'thoughtless delicate completeness', he shivers, concluding gently and firmly that love 'continues till we fail'. That failure will come and until then the dialectical process will go on 'ordeal/Succeeding ordeal till we find some death'. Failure—death—comes, when that self-enriching, forward-moving process is inhibited by their 'Hoarding bitterness, or refusing the cup'.

> Then the vivifying eye clouds, and the thin
> Mathematic tissues loosen, and the cup
> Thickens, and order dulls and dies in love's death
> And melts away in a hungerless no dream.

At this point, moved by these converging relationships between metaphysics, love and the beloved's luminous presence, the poem rises to a brief, intense hymn of praise to the beloved. The lover now offers her 'something for singing', released from the sour present, transcending the autumnal saturation.

> *Fragility echoing fragilities*
> *From whom I have had every distinctness*
> *Accommodate me still, where—folded in peace*
> *And undergoing with ghostly gaiety*
> *Inner immolation, shallowly breathing—*
>
> *You approach the centre by its own sweet light.*
> *I consign my designing will stonily*
> *To your flames. Wrapped in that rosy fleece, two lives*
> *Burn down around one love, one flickering-eyed*
> *Stone self becomes more patient than its own stone.*

This lyric appeals to her to continue to support him, identifying her as the source of his discoveries of order. She, by contrast with his frenetic struggle, is naturally in tune with the metaphysical texture he has defined. She is 'folded in peace', absorbed in a saint-like way in the process of transmuting successive ordeals. For him the devouring quality of life produces the calm he has mystically apprehended earlier in the poem. She burns with a phoenix-like flame and now, in startling contrast with the tone and imagery of *Wormwood*, he dedicates himself to her flames: clearly, as in the hospital, she symbolizes, indeed is a living embodiment of, life's ordeals accepted and transmuted. To her he consigns his 'designing will', abandoning any wish to impose order in favour of eliciting order now and in the future. The concluding lines outline the imagery of the bird consumed by fire, yet miraculously resurrected again from the process of destruction, magically recreated within the very force that destroys, and therefore an exact symbol for his own concept of art. Instead of 'Wormwood's' locked agony of scarred, twisted trunks, we have the Yeatsian-Swedenborgian union of flames. Joined in 'that rosy fleece' they endure the reduction of the body brought on by time's passing, but not overcome by a sense of bitterness and anguish, not figures in a dark comedy, but 'patient', resigned, triumphant.

Section III concludes on a note of resignation and acceptance. Issues of departure or return, change and renewal no longer harrow them. Choice is no longer agonizing, for the simple reason that they can accept either way: 'the ways are one, sweet choise/ *Our selves become our own best sacrifice'* (note 2).

Section IV: Stanzas 35-45

The poem rises in the final section to a happier tone. The lovers return through Phoenix Park, attended by propitious images, beauty flooding into the poem to replace autumnal damp, movement itself happy and joyful:

> The tires are singing, cornering back and forth
> In our green world again; into groves of trees,
> By lake and open park, past the hospital
> The west ignites behind us; ...

Ahead of them Dublin is a shimmer of life, movement, the glittering of spires in the evening sunlight 'Above faint multitudes'. The poem quickly condemns the city's theatrical waste and in one inclusive sweep scorns the lifeless quality of the people and their doings: 'And there dead men,/Half hindered by dead men, tear down dead beauty.'

Memories of their past, their courtship and consummation of love return as they re-enter the city. Love's fulfilment is also a union of opposites, male and female, but at the same time it is a liberation for the poet of his creative talents. Sexual intercourse releases his past into poetry, but in a narrower sense he has also incarnated in her. The last phantasm of the poem failed to achieve such liberation. But the giving of the body's seed is to be 'born' and brought to being, 'made whole'.

The 'one midnight' and 'room' refer to 'Baggot Street Deserta', before the beloved entered his life. He is about to begin the whole evolutionary-poetic process again, as he seeks to impregnate the womb of the imagination. In the final stanza he is on the verge of artistic utterance; from the depths below consciousness, the 'void', his words measure up to the triple darkness. The ordering processes of the imagination prepare the next poem: 'Delicate distinct tissue begins to form.'

CHAPTER 4

NEW POEMS (1973) and ONE (1974)

The epigraph to *Notes From The Land of the Dead* is drawn verbatim from the concluding lines of 'Phoenix Park':

> A snake out of the void moves in my mouth, sucks
> at triple darkness. A few ancient faces
> detach and begin to circle. Deeper still,
> delicate distinct tissue begins to form.

But, as a radical exploration of areas of the self below the conscious levels of thought, the poem, or sequence of poems, is closer in method and direction to 'Nightwalker' than to 'Phoenix Park'. The opening section, to which the above lines are introductory, stresses the extreme nature of the experience about to be described, how 'far and deep/ how long and cruel'. The speaker presents his material in retrospection, as an experience through which he has come and which has transformed him and his way of life. That former self and its time are affectionately mocked as a period of 'disarray', of 'dust', of frustrated search. But the descent to the land of the dead, the underworld of the self, the dark backward and abysm of time, is a journey 'out of my mind', a turning 'to things not right nor reasonable', Faustian, to an area or state where 'Time, distance' mean nothing. The metaphor of descent, of falling, pervades the book, involves a lapse from normal references of place and time, leads to encounters with or the liberation of inarticulate feelings and desires, to meetings with figures from the familial past, to a nightmare world of darkness and mystery. But the experience is beneficent and restorative. The archetypal journey to the underworld, to areas of deepest discovery, ultimately proves redemptive. The fearful fall through the iron grating or shore, the breaking of the shell and the releasing into liquid fragments are metaphors for the radical and absolute exploration, and the renewal that the poem itself projects and that the book of poems takes as its central drama. The 'pit' to which he drops 'So far from the world and earth...' is an area of becoming, of 'wavery albumen bodies' in which, having broken free from former shapes and conditions, a new potential may be realized, or in which any new combination of tissues may achieve a delicate distinctness. Here the 'naked ancient women' with 'limp talons' prefigure later encounters with polymorphous female figures, taloned, cruel, flesh-eating, birds of prey, gorgon creatures or owls. Above him is 'that seemingly unattainable grill' through which he must return, carrying his 'prize'. The speaker's attitude here is consciously dramatic as a result of his feeling that what he has to relate is so unusual and his memory of it so fragmentary that he will not be believed. His manner is colloquial, his theme extraordinary, but he swears to its truth.

In 'Invocation' the encounter with the female figure is sexual, a vision of that union of the potential elements, the 'living particles' with the 'living blossom' of a creative hunger.

> —cells of ruby blood, jewels
> to kiss and melt; crystal eyes
> to fasten against, fluttering; pink tongues
> to cling lingering among—

Allusion in this poem to the rape of Proserpina, the general underworld setting for the book, the references to eating pip-filled fruit, to owl figures, the thrust of the book from darkness to light, from the land of the dead to the land of the living, and the creation myths to be found in some of the poems, all suggest a primordial mythological level in *Notes From The Land of the Dead*. The myth of Proserpina's rape by Pluto, the search by Ceres, goddess of corn-bearing earth, the final agreement that her daughter should spend a portion of the year in the underworld with Pluto and a portion of it with her mother, symbolize a vegetation myth and in a deeper sense man's death and future life. The poppies picked by Proserpina are also a promise of resurrection after death—in 'Invocation' the speaker cries out to be plucked—and the pomegranate she has actually eaten in Hades has sprung from the blood of Adonis. Furthermore, when Ascalaphus tells about her having eaten this fruit, he is turned into an owl.

In the encounters presented in these poems the idea of stasis is frequent; the moment sharply recalled from the past or vividly seen in dream or reverie is not understood. Clarity imposes an intensity of significance on the moment in itself, but the poem's inner movement is not towards insight, but towards a heightened and memorable apprehension. 'Hen Woman' provides a dramatic tableau, arresting the flow of time and action, like figures in a still photograph. In the hushed moment the egg emerging from the hen, the woman emerged from the cottage out of the 'black hole', the hot noon stillness, the 'locked' gaze of the observer, are all part of a hypnotic moment, a 'mystery' in which 'time stood still' and 'Nothing moved'. The 'tiny and mechanical' beetle carrying the ball of dung signifies the potential, the substance in which life may begin, as well as the waste of death. The egg falling slowly, dreamlike, and breaking through the grating recalls the fall of the opening poem, the descent towards death and all similar descents in these poems. For the observer, the 'I' figure, the emphasis is not on what meanings he may derive from the scene, but on the tenacity of such memories—('I had felt all this before'). As part of a human experience, the scene is even comical, but as part of Kinsella's metaphysic it is of great importance.

> I feed upon it still, as you see;
> there is no end to that which,
> not understood, may yet be noted

and hoarded in the imagination,
in the yolk of one's being, so to speak,
there to undergo its (quite animal) growth,
dividing blindly;
twitching, packed with will,
searching in its own tissue
for the structure
in which it may wake.
Something that had—clenched
in its cave—not been
now was: an egg of being.
Through what seemed a whole year it fell
—as it still falls, for me,
solid and light, the red gold beating
in its silvery womb,
alive as the yolk and white
of my eye: as it will continue
to fall, probably, until I die,
through the vast indifferent spaces
with which I am empty.

Several poems return to childhood experience, in particular
to encounters with the figure of the ancient grandmother. In
'A Hand of Solo' she is the source of knowledge, offering him
the tempting pomegranate, a three-headed Hecate figure. The
associations of these old female figures are consistent—
darkness, sour or stale smell, an abyss, back room, a taloned
image or accompanying flesh-eating bird. In her presence the
child faces a challenge, as here where he accepts the
pomegranate, bites into it 'tasting the first traces of the
blood',

loosening the packed mass of dryish beads
from their indigo darkness.
I drove my tongue among them

and took a mouthful, and slowly
bolted them. My throat filled
with a rank, Arab bloodstain.

That final moment is linked with the opening section where the self experiences a love-relationship, both maternal and sexual, in images of delicious eating. 'Ancestor' is a portrait of this woman whose profile 'was old, and dark like a hunting bird's'; she too is surrounded by a distinctive, unusual smell; she too has a key, moves in darkness 'among sweet- and fruit-boxes', dwells behind 'red hangings' in the 'back room'. It is through such attendant and defining details that he goes in 'Tear' to say goodbye to her on her deathbed, carried in the process 'to unfathomable depths'. The scene is remembered with intense clarity, with its fear that she might tempt him 'with open mouth'

> to hide myself one last time
> against her, and bury my
> self in her drying mud.

The farewell kiss he transfers to 'the chill/ and smell' of her 'black aprons'. The effect is to carry him by association to a 'derelict place/smelling of ash'. This direct contact with death is alleviated by a memory of the tears his father shed at the death of a small sister. What he tastes now, instead of ash, is the compassionate heart of the dying woman, moved by her son's grief for the loss of a child. At the heart of this darkness, where terror and mystery dwell,—her heart beating 'now' is horrified—he has found what he was looking for

> —not heat nor fire,
> nor any comfort,
>
> but her voice, soft, talking to someone
> about my father....

Understanding is gained by facing the aged woman and the fears associated with her, an understanding of life's cruel ordeals, a wider sense of life and death, and a respect for the capacity of old people to 'digest' experience. It is wholly characteristic of these poems that the two central figures of the grandmother and the boy do not communicate. Each concentrates on her or his own experience. Similarly in the meeting of the moon figure with Endymion, in the poem of that title, the contact yields but a blaze of light which is caused by their meeting. This short poem might be taken as paradigmatic for several poems in this book. It begins 'At first there was nothing' and this is what actually survives the meeting. In any terms there has been no change, no perceptive or intended alteration in the two figures or in the context in which they meet. The 'single drop' echoing in the 'depths' is like the momentary blaze of light at the meeting of the two figures, but the emphasis here, and in the other poems, is on the vast distance between the two.

In 'The High Road' the boy sets out after a visit to the grandmother figure, giver of 'A silvery/ little mandoline, out of the sweet-box'. The poem moves through precisely noted details of place, things and people, to the quiet admission that his vision of things past is wholly unsentimental, not something to be lyrical about. Here his fearful descent to the pit brings a bleak notation:

> it was only a hollow someone made,
> with a dusty piece of man's dung
> and a few papers in a corner,
> and bluebottles.

On the high road he remembers that conclusion to his earlier quest. The sense of loss at the end of the poem is for that childhood realization of dust and waste. The silvery strings of the tiny mandoline that trembled in his brain after his visit to the old woman do not tremble again, silenced by this landscape, with its details of 'stones and tin cans in the Camac', by its bleak vision of excrement and bluebottles. For all of this the mandoline is essentially unsuited. The incident recollected here is one of boyish adventure, when he climbed to the Robbers' Den; the contrast is between romantic conceptions of that Den and the actualities of the 'big hole'. At the conclusion he abandons his romantic instrument:

> and let it fall
> for ever into empty space
> ..., and saw it turn
> over with a tiny flash,
> silvery shivering with loss.

The poems in Section II stress the chasm between the boy and the grandmother and what each stands for. By exploring the chasm in mythical or allegorical terms, they provide an understanding of what is involved in the conjunction of the two figures. 'Nuchal' stands at one end of the long road that leads from one to the other. This picture of the smiling, ladylike woman, the brilliant pure water, the four dividing streams is a dream conception of the female figure, 'monstrous' because so long-lasting, so fundamental and so out of touch with the other end of the perspective, 'that bitter river' towards which all the others flow. The sensuously descriptive language of this poem and its rich decorative texture contrast strongly with the linguistic mode, the hesitant rhythm, the appalled tone that exist in many of the other poems in the book.

The complex differences between woman and child are taken up in 'Survivor', which approaches the qualities of that chasm in several ways. 'Nuchal' presented an Edenic world: its four rivers from *Genesis 2*, are also found in *Lebor Gabala Erenn*, where the spring of Paradise from which they flow is called 'Nuchal' (note 1). 'Survivor' also draws upon the latter. The survivor-persona may be identified with Fintan, one of the three men who arrived in Ireland with the prediluvian Cessair and her company of women. When they threatened him, he took refuge on the Hill of the Wave where he sheltered in a cave and survived the Flood. As the one who lived to tell the tale he resembles the persona of the introductory poem in *Notes From the Land of the Dead*, another survivor from the land of the dead. Cessair's people were also regarded as thieves; she and her followers were excluded from the Ark by Noah for this reason. In some

87

accounts the early peoples were thought to have come from the sky, or from the ocean. The poem touches lightly and suggestively on these and other elements from *Lebor Gabala*, such as references to the East, the search for an earthly paradise, the sickness that overtakes them, the Hag Rock, and the ambiguous nature of the place. Paradoxically, in Celtic mythology Munster is both the land of the dead and the place of origins, which makes it perfectly appropriate for Kinsella's purposes here. 'Survivor' implicitly suggests the emergent possibilities, but places greater emphasis on the barren chasm within the rock. *Finistère*, however, affirms the arrival in Ireland as a state of promise: out of the burial megaliths a new civilization is created (note 2).

The 'cavern' or 'cave' of the poem is the place of life and death also, 'our first home', a place of origin, endurance and survival, the rock from which the voice of the narrator comes and within which the unconscious may be detected. But the recurrent pattern of the poem is of movement from promise to failure; the earthly paradise becomes a place of 'gloom', the sinless land a place of violence, with 'otherworldly music' — 'A land of the dead'. The myth of promise becomes a reality of despair; the poem sinks to an abysmal emotional state. For the chasm also involves the inability to feel, the withdrawal of response, a numbness. Vaguely, in this otherworld state, there lingers a memory of a better state—'a thin thread of some kind of sweetness'—but it is over-shadowed by a different memory, of abuse and terror, of possibilities that were cruelly checked. The poem moves here, from these disrupted echoes of things past, to a more definite recollection of a 'fair beginning', the 'entire new world' anticipated and lost, or at least changed in quality from what had been envisaged. The descriptions of the pristine land and the joyful progress towards it alter to an account of the reality: the land of the dead dominated by the 'she-wolf'. The conditions here—sickness, twilight, the great rock called 'The Hag' pointing 'up at nothing'—are familiar images of barrenness, pain and decay. The poem ends bleakly:

> There is nothing here for sustenance.
> Unbroken sleep were best.
> Hair. Claws. Grey.
> Naked. Wretch. Wither.

The speaker, the mythical survivor of the title, endures in these conditions, determined to 'remember' and 'to explain'.

In terms of that vast experience that lies between the two figures, this poem 'Survivor' is a drama of loss, of the exclusion from fair beginnings into a state of masochistic inertia and into an existence of utter waste, a nothingness. The differences between the two figures are further developed in 'At the Crossroads' in the presentation of a choice that has to be made. The three separate yet similar metaphors of a definite yet indistinct threat, each associated with Hecate, correspond to the fear involved in the choice. But the nature of the risk is first seen in the white face of the moon staring down from the void and is given full actuality in the fiercely predatory activity, and rounded off when the owl lifts off to the tree 'with blackness in her heart'. That is the 'choice', the swift, passionate response, the lesson already offered by the grandmother in the pomegranate. The boy's consumption of the fruit corresponds exactly to the owl's attack in this poem. Failure to make that choice leaves one in the frozen state of the figure in 'Survivor'.

The most radical use of the eating metaphor comes in 'Sacrifice', which begins as a description of a sacrificial killing joyfully engaged in by the victim's friend, but shifts excitedly to an identification with the victim as she co-operates ecstatically with her killers—'I've never felt/ so terribly alive, so ready, so gripped by love'. In this symbolic enactment, the fear of the last poem has been transcended; instead of inertia and hopelessness, there is purpose and passion. Beyond pain, once the choice has been made, lies the satisfaction of total possession by another and the fulfilment and knowledge to be found, the ultimate communication.

> We are each other's knowledge. It is peace that counts,
> and knowledge brings peace, even thrust crackling

into the skull and bursting with tongues of fire.
Peace. Love dying down, as love ascends.

I love your tender triumph, straightening up,
lifting your reddened sleeves. The stain spreads downward
through your great flushed pinions.
You are a real angel.
My heart is in your hands: mind it well.

The moment stands out from the poems in this section in its tone of confidence. Those elements of pain, fear and loss in the preceding poems, including the idealized world of 'Nuchal' are here transmuted into pleasure and love. Even the associations of rock and claw are changed, as the predatory female, the threatening owl, are transformed into the phoenix rising from the flame and becoming an angel. The ambiguous blend of good and evil, swan and snake found at the end of 'Downstream' is repeated here in the terminology of 'Phoenix Park', in a radiant and unified image also won out of darkness and fear.

Notes From the Land of the Dead is a sequence of poems in the strict sense, because each poem therein gains in significance from its relationship to and interaction with other poems in the book, and any one poem, taken by itself, loses much of its force. Just as the female figures are demonstrably the same figure in successive poems, defined by recurrent associations of darkness, smell, death and predatory birds, so the book as a whole is permeated by basic objects, images, and incidents that interact with each other in a meaningful and enriching manner. Some of the primary incidents are those of encounter: boy with grandmother, Endymion with the moon figure, owls with their victims, the speaker with his varied environment. Closely allied with this encounter is the fall or movement to another kind of world, out of normal surroundings or responses, towards a new and often dangerous experience. The book itself may be said to be situated in darkness, or Night, in a void so that one of its primary and motivating concerns is with beginnings, the first flickers of formative factors, sometimes barely sensed. The idea of a place or state out of the time-space continuum is inferred in references to pit, abyss, cavern, cave, orifice, shore and their associated images. Again, closely related with these are those indications of potential, a musical sound, a tear, a drop of moisture, an echo, and it seems any reference to water or liquid; these all signal release or, at least, the possibility of change, although they must always be assessed within the contexts. Most visible are the female figures, sometimes like spirits, sometimes actual: the grandmother figures, owls, Hecate, Proserpina, the dreamlike lady of 'Nuchal', the ecstatic victim of 'Sacrifice', the predatory creatures. One of the risks involved in separating these basic images, objects and incidents is that at the deepest level they coalesce into one complex meaning. Indeed, the difficulty in dealing with *Notes From the Land of the Dead* is that the necessary simplification that goes with interpretation and comment denies the poems their freight of interfusion and endless complication.

The way in which a poem gains in meaning through the operation and accumulated power of these recurrent meanings may be seen in the first poem of Section III which is entitled 'All Is Emptiness, And I Must Spin'. The general mood of this third section is of recovery based on and achieved within the void:

> A vacancy in which, apparently
> I hang,
>   with severed senses

and despite the unsuitability of the rational faculty,

> How bring oneself to judge, or think,
> so hurled onward!
>   inward!

In the changed attitude of this section darkness is 'not Death, but Night...' within which there is a 'dew on the face/ tears of self forming'. Within the 'cavern', amid the 'darkness', and despite the taste of 'ash', there is the 'echo'. Because of the meanings these terms have already acquired, the poem is enabled to move quietly and firmly to its seemingly amazing, even absurd conclusion:

> The sterile: it is a whole matter in itself.
> Fantastic millions of
> fragile
>
> in every single

Notes From the Land of the Dead deals with beginnings, with the 'emptiness' which sometimes comes. By this third section the challenge and the many meanings of the land of the dead have been accepted. Within waste and ash, in the darkness, where death holds sway, may be found multiple particles engaged in their natural activities: 'Solid matter', as the poem 'Ely Place' says in a different context, 'flickering in broad daylight'. Finally, it must be observed that these encounters with the mysterious, the unknowable, the threatening, as well as with the infinite and complex congruences of matter, are primarily experiences private to the poet, the 'I' figure. Although at first the emphasis seems to be on the boy and the old woman crusted with knowledge, the real concern is with the self, with the whole process of growth and how we learn. In that larger dimension, boy and woman are points on the scale. Those poems that conjoin the two create a radical contrast. He stands on the threshold of the road; she at the end. What he finds in her, could he but digest it all, is his own future, himself at later stages. Her great age as she is about to go into oblivion serves as a foil to his great innocence. What he buys from her in the pomegranate is knowledge of life and death, truth, love, peace, the example of her proven capacity for the absorption of life. Paradoxically, therefore, it is in her, in her proximity to death and darkness, in her imminent descent to oblivion, lies a way into life, a birth. Through his nauseating contact with her drying mud he finds her heart beating in his mouth, that is, her ability to bite into experience. She is the pungent source of knowledge. As the archetypal underworld journey also says, in death we find life; the two extreme points on the road between boy and woman come to the same thing. In the chasm that exists between them, with all that it is made to imply in the course of these poems, lies life.

Unless we have grasped this cohesive fact, the final poem becomes almost incomprehensible. The night world of the book, its darkness and waste, the sense of loss, the descent to the underworld, become positive. Within the barren mountain lie the cavern and the lingering myth of human origins. The rock is the womb.

> if you look closely
> you can see the tender undermost
> muscle actually forming
> from the rock, and the living veins
> continuing inward, just visible
> under the skin, and (faintly lit from within)
> clusters of soft arms gathering down
> tiny open eyes, finger tips, pursed mouths,
> down from the gloom, minute
> drifting corruscations of light, glistening
> little gnat-crescents of hair!

The imaginative intensity of this embryonic condition comes from this penetration of the rock, this reaching downwards into the darkness, the seemingly impossible areas, in the faith that nothing is alien to the imagination, nothing is outside its reach. Beyond, below, in the 'profounder nothingness' there are 'essences'— 'flickering, delicate/ and distinct'.

'Good Night', the final poem, is a poetic statement of that redemption, made in the book's own imaginal patterns of night, darkness, feeding, the state of unknowing in which the speaker, intensely alert and malleable, brings back his prize, his incredible truth. He is 'Attached into the darkness by every sense':

> fingers and tongue
>   outstretched—
> into a nothingness
> inhabited by a vague animal light
> from the walls and floor.

The dense last section of the poem reiterates in its convoluted
phrases a metaphor of a confusion of substance that is at the
same time a certainty, though of a different order from those
truths and certainties available to the rational part of the self.
Kinsella's sense of living substance within the deepest recesses
of the psyche is an instinctive response based on an
imaginative faith. The 'monsters' and 'voices', the feeding,
the coiling and uncoiling, gather together in a parasitic and
creative activity, in that complex confusion of matter within
which potentiality lies. Experience absorbed or digested
becomes part of the psyche, feeding upon it, inseparable
from it, a nourishment for it.

> daylit, we are the monsters of our night,
> and somewhere the monsters of our night are ...
> here ... in the daylight that our nightnothing
> feeds in and feeds, wandering
> out of the cavern, a low cry
> echoing—Camacamacamac...
>
> that we need as we don't need truth...
>
> and ungulfs a Good Night, smiling.

In these compressed references to those basic images that
have found meaning in earlier poems, this final poem restates
the paradoxical identity of night and day, reaffirms the
possibility of potential leading to a birth. The reappearance
of the 'brown' Camac, one of Dublin's famous underground
rivers already seen in 'The High Road', is also a positive note.
Instead of the tiny mandoline, there is this echo from the
cavern and the final affirmation that these elemental acts of

faith are more important than 'truth', because more fundamental, and that out of the underworld, out of the land of
the dead, comes 'a Good Night'.

*

Other poems in this collection are closely related to those in
Notes From the Land of the Dead in theme and attitude.
Their general concern is with the hidden and inexplicable
ways of growth and the concomitant feeling about the
finitude of human perception and understanding. In 'The
Route of the Táin' the way lies 'over men's dust' towards hills
that grow darker as they are approached. In contrast to the
various confusions that beset the modern travellers, the old
way is certified in the topography of the land. The inability
of the contemporary travellers to handle their own emotional
instability is also solved in the natural setting when the fox
races across the ridge and points them in the right direction.
The pointer is more metaphysical than geographical.

> the process, the whole tedious
> enabling ritual! Flux brought to fullness
> —saturated—the clouding over—dissatisfaction
> spreading slowly like an ache: something
> reduced shivering suddenly into meaning
> along new boundaries

Human frailty does not inhibit the poem's free and confident
growth from frustration through unexpected natural confirmation towards the regrouping of the last lines. The irony of
writing poems about human uncertainty in a highly skilful
way is one of the particular delights of these poems. Other
reflections on human limitations are 'Drowsing over the
Arabian Nights', 'Death Bed', 'The Clearing' and the elegiac
A Selected Life.
The elegy for the composer and musician Seán O Riada
begins with a portrait of an artist perfectly in tune with his
medium: the imagery of an animal alertness and response

makes a physical attitude reveal the inner force. The shift of focus to the funeral accentuates the loss occasioned by his premature death, his separation from the 'essentials' of family, music, unfinished work, all of which suffer the deprivation of his going. The poem uses simple particulars of the day's events to convey in this simplicity of detail and reference and in its mute objectivity the inconsolable reality of death. The rain, the ominous flesh-eating crow, the dead rat, the remote body not yet in the grave fit into a total picture of a man once intensely fulfilled in the correspondence of artist and craft, now bluntly removed. After a single tender memory of him as a Pierrot in the sun, the poem, selective in its details, bluntly summarizes the life and the death.

> swallowed back: animus
> brewed in clay, uttered
> in brief meat and brains, and flattened
> back under our flowers.

Sadly, gently, with a dignity in keeping with the poem's classic simplicity and decorum, the last lines, in which the voices of poet and composer alternate, pay affectionate salute and farewell.

That affectionate note sounds more clearly in the sophisticated sequel, *Vertical Man*, in which the blunt objectivity of *A Selected Life* is replaced by an intimate encounter with the ghostly presence of the dead composer. By sharing his concept of the artistic processes, Kinsella conveys the affinity of taste and sensibility that existed between poet and composer. Furthermore, paying his friend the tribute of imitation, he intensifies and deepens this part of the elegy with his allusions to Gustav Mahler's *Das Lied von der Erde*, Seán O Riada's recording, *Vertical Man*, and the poem *Das Trinklied vom Jammer der Erde* by Hans Bethge, upon which both musical works are partially based and which Kinsella here modifies and adapts for his own elegiac purposes. Finally, by means of Bethge's allusion to the ape-figure howling above the grave, he shifts to the redeeming song of the fisherman in 'The Shoals Returning' who in the exercise of his 'gift' could prepare the human spirit for death. In that conclusion the work of poet and composer finds its true 'reward'.

The resonant interplay of literary and musical allusions in *Vertical Man* is in keeping with Kinsella's recent uses of secondary sources. 'St Paul's Rocks' is derived almost entirely from Darwin's account of them in *The Voyage of the Beagle*, 'Death Bed' draws upon Thomas Mann's account of the death of Jacob, 'The Dispossessed' upon Ernest Renan's *Vie de Jesus*, and 'Drowsing Over the Arabian Nights' upon one of the lesser tales. But the technique is used more intricately in *The Good Fight: a poem for the tenth anniversary of the death of John F. Kennedy* (1973), which makes use of selections from Kennedy speeches, biographies, news reports, a song of the New Frontier, Plato, an article on Lee Harvey Oswald, and Oswald's diary. The success of the poem depends largely on the effective interplay of these diverse elements.

Central to this dynamic world is the question of causality. Kennedy and Oswald are both 'vessels of decision', the one massing a generation about him with his idealistic vision of social and cultural renewal, the other lonely, isolated and nihilistic, and compelled towards action. That their paths should have crossed so unpredictably and so disastrously makes Plato's concepts of social and human behaviour questionable, even peripheral. His statements fall like choric commentary into this drama of the rational and the irrational; his articulations of justice do not explain or confirm the actuality of experience. The result is that the poem moves within and towards questions: Kennedy's dying question as imagined by Oswald, Oswald's tentative nihilism, the public's bewilderment at the assassination, the poet's possibility of understanding. Robert Frost's bleak conclusion that all *un*reasonable things are possible and that *everything* that can happen will happen is qualified in the poem's final section. The poem itself, registering this variety of emphasis and response, illustrates its own conclusion in that mode of registering. The poem lets things *'be'* so that its meaning, unlike Plato's natural theology, lies in the imaginative truth within its resonant assembly of elements. In contrast with Plato's faith in such qualities as balance, apportionment, harmony, the dance, in 'our secondary world' the possibility of understanding gained through acceptance remains. Events may, as the poem indicates, frustrate logic and one's sense of justice, may indeed deny Plato's idealistic point of view, but Kinsella's faith in the values of the rational imagination is unshaken.

> it is we, letting things *be*,
> who might come at understanding.
> That is the source of our patience.

Kinsella's approach in the elegy is unsentimental; there is no heightening of the emotion, no rhetorical flourish. The 'passion', as the artist figure in 'Worker in Mirror, at His Bench' explains, 'is in the putting together'.

> I tinker with the things that dominate me,
> as they describe their random
> persistent coherences...
> clear surfaces shift
> and glitter among themselves

It is, he says, a question of

> easing the particular of its litter,
> bending attention on the remaining depths
> as though questions had never been....

The interdependence of things in nature is an analogue for the ways in which poems emerge. *Notes From the Land of the Dead* works by symbiosis; much of its significance is symbolical of the coalescence within the poet from which poems come into being. In a different way and at deeper levels than 'Phoenix Park', the book is also a quest for creativity and a manifestation of the success of that quest. 'Worker in Mirror, at His Bench' goes behind the scenes to consider the artist at his task. What begins as a jocular, conversational poem, with social dimensions, ends as a stark expression of the isolation of the artist and the horror of his inner vision. As in the elegy, the poem declares that the act of engagement with the material from which a poem is produced is a natural and satisfying relationship.

> The bright assembly begins to turn in silence.
> The answering brain glitters—one system
> answering another.   The senses enter
> and reach out with a pulse of pleasure
> to the four corners of their own wilderness.

But these correspondences give way to the four diminishing masks. Their declension from gold to silver to bronze ends in Kinsella country where the one brilliant head now dark as iron is concentrated into 'two blazing eyes' and one 'wolf-muzzle': a ravenous predator whose 'unholy tongue laps, tastes/ brothers' thick blood'. His engagement with the material however carried him even further, inward to a horrifying image of yet another head, at a lower point in this declension, absorbing the whole time-space continuum and the whole of life.

> blackness—all matter
> in one light-devouring
> polished cliff-face
> hurtling rigid
> from zenith to pit
> through dead

As against that ultimate state may be placed those poems which deal more positively with man's hunger for life and for understanding. 'Death Bed' is a poignant account of this longing for understanding:

Our people are most vulnerable to loss
when we gather like this to one side
around some death,

and try to weave it into our lives
—who can weave nothing but our ragged
routes across the desert.

And it is those among us
who most make the heavens their business
who go most deeply into this death-weaving.

As if the star might
spring from the dying mouth
or shoot from the agony of the eyes.

'We must not miss it,
however it comes'.
—If it comes.

What Kinsella brings to these poems is an acceptance of life
as he finds it, without distracting or spurious consolations,
and without the ethic of suffering that he had once
advocated rather severely. Idealizations must also go; the
golden and silver images have their surrogate in the wolfhead.
Similarly the idyllic world of 'The Dispossessed' in which the
godlike figure lifts 'His unmangled hand' must be rejected
because the concept of the divine involves 'humiliation'; the
more intense the notion of the ideal, the greater the
degradation.

These beauties,
these earth flowers growing and blowing, what are they?
The spectacle of your humiliation!

That tone of contempt and of authoritarian will finds no
place in Kinsella's primitive feeling about those forces that
actually propel the world. His detachment has become more

comprehensive. In addition, the cool gaze of the poet has become more identifiable with the scrutiny of the naturalist. He had always been a naturalist at heart. His early preference was for a career as a naturalist, his favourite reading had been works of natural science, his attraction to de Chardin was logical as well as imaginative. But his idea of the onward turbulence of forms was restricted in that it was fitted to his rigorous idea of advancement through suffering. Now, while still responsive to that movement towards the void, his view is less shadowed by the 'blight'. Two poems, in particular, in this new collection, embody his more balanced attitude: 'St Paul's Rocks' and 'Crab Orchard Sanctuary: Late October'. The former calls attention to the natural miracle of symbiosis:

> Colonies of birds eat the abundant fish;
> moths feed on the feathers, lice and beetles
> live in the dung, countless spiders
> prey on these scavengers; in the crevices
> a race of crabs lives on the eggs and young.
>
> In squalor and killing and parasitic things
> life takes its first hold.

The tension in these poems lies between the perception of a dense world of Darwinian reality and a sense of death in the midst of life. The balance struck between the two makes for the kind of poem that absorbs the natural world in its rich profusion even as it attests to its provisional grace. The eye of the naturalist is perfectly adjusted to see the plenitude of the actual, as well as the squalor and the cruelty. Life, including imaginative life, takes its hold in just such a rich assembly. Later comes the 'noble accident' of the seed falling where it will find sustenance.

'Crab Orchard Sanctuary: Late October' is an elegy of a kind; all the precise notations of its first section, and the gentle rhythms and images of evanescence, portray the autumnal scene. The illusion of stasis, the ominous hush, the dreamy rise and fall of the lake water, the fragile loveliness of the spider silk blowing 'softly from the tips of the trees', the Indian metamorphosed in the distance, the far perspectives, the geese 'settling in', are all part of the same natural text. The poet's lingering watch, a solitary observer of a deserted scene, unites his pleasure in its beauties with regret for their impermanence.

That duality of response comes from an earlier watching in which the quails and the diminishing wasps and crickets have underlined the natural cycle. Therefore against the afternoon's sad delight he would set the morning's drama:

> Hidden everywhere, a myriad
> leather seed-cases lie in wait
> nourishing curled worms of white fat
> —ugly, in absolute certainty, piteous,
> threatening in every rustling sound:
>   bushes worrying in the night breeze,
> dry leaves detaching, and creeping.
> They will swarm again, on suffocated nights,
> with their endless hysterics; and wither away again.

Given that hideous certainty he would ask a rhetorical question, directed as much to himself as to others, about those who 'stand still' watching and listening, as he has in the first section. Given that threat in the very centre of things, including the 'glittering' and 'withering' brain of the watcher what is to be done? The answer lies in the poem itself which counters, even as it fully incorporates, the 'slow hot glare/ spreading on the water'. Who will watch

> the erratic jays and cardinals flashing
> blue and red among the branches and trunks

Who, it might be asked in reply, would deny himself the value of such watching simply because what he sees will not last and because he too is mortal?

*

An answer may be seen elsewhere, in the long poem
Finistère, published in 1972 but not included in *New Poems*.
This account of the journey of a race of people, the Sons of
Mil, from Finistère in Brittany to the borders of the then
known world in Ireland, another *finisterre*, is an otherworld
journey in reverse, a coming into being. It is also an
affirmation of man's insatiable hunger for the new possibility. In its deliberate use of Amhairgin's song from *Lebor
Gabala*, in which he claims to subsume all existence in
himself, it is a declaration of belief in poetry, as well as in
man's creative spirit.

Who
    is the bull with seven stars
    the hawk on the cliff
    the salmon sunk in his pool
    the pool sunk in her soil
    the animal's fury
    the flower's fibre
    a teardrop in the sun?

Like the descents in *Notes From the Land of the Dead*, this
oceanic journey through 'salt chaos' is the result of an inner
'unrest' and an inward progress. Its ending resembles and
contains its beginning. These voyagers are moved by their
need to reach out beyond the known, but also by a racial
memory. Their mental images of what they will find in
Ireland indicate both the civilization they will create there,
the civilization they have formed in Brittany, and the
memory of the one their ancestors built in Northern Spain,
another Finistère, another civilization made by megalith-
builders. In addition, what is anticipated as a movement
towards the sunlight becomes a movement into death, into
the burial chambers of the Boyne Valley into which the sun's
rays also reach at the winter solstice. The spirals, lozenge and
zigzag patterns on the stone slabs of Newgrange, already

103

present in their minds, render in their self-enclosed and impenetrable design the mysterious and unknowable both within the self and in the world outside.

> poolspirals opening on
> closing spiralpools
> and dances drilled in the rock
> in coil zigzag angle and curl
> river ripple earth ramp
> suncircle moonloop...

The narrator of *Finistère*, already identified with Amhairgin in his cosmic vision of things interrelated and available to him, also proclaims his need and urge to absorb the whole:

> Who goes in full into
> the moon's interesting conditions?
> who fingers the sun's sink hole?
> (I went forward, reaching out)

The cosmological aspects of *Finistère*, although belonging to the original account in the *Book of Invasions (Lebor Gabala)* of the arrival in Ireland of the sons of Mil, are quite in keeping with Kinsella's own tendency to expand his material towards the cosmic and universal.

One (1974), which includes 'Finistère', is closely related to *Notes From the Land of the Dead* in its concern with source, in its reiterative method, in the kinds of material used. But the potential of section III is now a more positive force, embodied in more fully realised metaphors, and infused in the idiom and texture of the poetry. In their progress towards specific revelations, the poems themselves enact the dynamic of possibility, in the language of change and movement—things flickering, squirming, hissing, beating—in ghostly presences and ancestors, and through their metaphysical penetrations of the barriers of time, space and matter. Nightmare, hallucination and dread may still accompany these explorations, but as means of discovery, and the emphasis—through tone, language and organisation—is on the possibilities of source, the availability of redemption.

Growth and renewal are manifested in the interaction of past and present, in the heritage of time, in the very nature of things. In 'Finistère' the generations are linked: 'whose excited blood was that/ fumbling our movements? Whose ghostly hunger/tunneling our thoughts full of passages...?' In 'Minstrel' the earth and the heavens become an epiphany of growth. In 'His Father's Hands' the abandoned block surviving through the years gives birth, beautifully, to its legacy:

> it turned under my hands, an axis
> of light flashing down its length,
> and the wood's soft flesh broke open,
> countless little nails
> squirming and dropping out of it.

Frequently the moment of insight has female associations. Even in '38 Phoenix Street' the Sacred Heart in the picture beats within 'women's fingers'; and in 'The Oldest Place' the standing stone has a shawled face.

The receiving consciousness in these poems yields to experience, trusting to 'evolutions or accidents', even as the voyagers in 'Finistère' respond to the complex forces within and to the cosmic elements. Repeatedly the poems echo and parallel motifs and directions from previous work, as far back as 'An Ancient Ballet' or 'Baggot Street Deserta'. What is by now evident is that Kinsella's work as a whole contains correspondences, not only from poem to poem within a particular book, but from book to book. There is a growing sense of continuity and of a unity of design.

*

Butcher's Dozen: A Lesson for the Octave of Widgery is a unique poem in the Kinsella canon in that it is public, satirical and occasional. Like *Finistère*, it was published in 1972 and was not included in *New Poems* although it is included in *Notes From the Land of the Dead and Other Poems* (1973). The immediate occasion was the publication of the report of the Widgery Tribunal which had been set up to investigate the killing of thirteen Civil Rights demonstrators in Derry on 30 January 1972 by British paratroopers, but the contempt and anger that run through it reflect a general rage in the south of Ireland. Lord Widgery, the Lord Chief Justice of England, issued the tribunal's report on 18 April 1972. Kinsella's verse pamphlet appeared on 26 April, 'within the octave'.

The poem's main device is to allow the words of the thirteen dead to contradict the spurious findings of the report. One example of this technique may be seen in what the tribunal called 'the special feature of Gerald Donaghy's case'. The report read as follows:

> The Medical Officer made a more detailed examination afterwards but on neither occasion did he notice anything unusual in Donaghy's pockets. After another short interval, and whilst Donaghy's body still lay on the back seat of Mr Rogan's car, it was noticed that he had a nail bomb in one of his trouser pockets (as photographed in RUC photographs EP5A/26 and 27). An Ammunition Technical Officer (Bomb Disposal Officer, Soldier 127) was sent for and found four nail bombs in Donaghy's pockets.(note 3)

In the poem the ghost of Gerald Donaghy derides the report in this manner:

> 'A bomber I. I travelled light
> —Four pounds of nails and gelignite
> About my person, hid so well
> They seemed to vanish where I fell.
> When the bullet stopped my breath
> A doctor sought the cause of death.

> He upped my shirt, undid my fly,
> Twice he moved my limbs awry,
> And noticed nothing. By and by
> A soldier, with his sharper eye,
> Beheld the four elusive rockets
> Stuffed in my coat and trouser pockets.
> Yes, they must be strict with us,
> Even in death so treacherous!'

Contempt is one motivating force. Another is indignation and amazement that the ruling classes in Britain and in Northern Ireland should have learnt so little from past mistakes. The anti-imperialist theme is sounded strongly in the poem in the accusation of exploitation, indifference to local traditions, repression, the creation of internal dissension, followed eventually by the condescending exit from a state left in ruin. That Unionists should nevertheless cling blindly to the English connection provokes this comic opera portrayal

> Sashed and bowler-hatted, glum
> Apprentices of fife and drum
> ...
> Drilled at the codeword 'True Religion'
> To strut and mutter like a pigeon
> 'Not an Inch—Up the Queen';

These mindless responses to empty formulas, to 'scribbled magic' are the final point in the poem's ascent from the immediate context of death and bloodshed in condemnation of the specific tribunal to the wider historical and moral perspectives. These universal aspects allow for the decline of indignation and invective to the parody of 'Pope and Devil intertwine' and the note of compassion with which the poem concludes. The transition here is from the rhetorical and dismissive 'Who could love them?' to the more compassionate response of the thirteenth corpse, 'Smiling in its bloody head', that 'pity is akin to love'. The appeal finally is to patience, to the principle that every nation has its rightful

107

place, to the reasonable plea that since the North is a 'mongrel' nation, like all others, it should be given a chance.

> At least let in
> A breath or two of oxygen,
> So they may settle down for good
> And mix themselves in the common blood.
> We are what we are, and that
> Is mongrel pure. What nation's not
> Where any stranger hung his hat
> And seized a lover where she sat?

CHAPTER 5

THE TAIN (1969)

No study of Kinsella's poetry would be complete without referring to his translation of the greatest Old Irish saga, *Táin Bó Cuailnge* and some of its related stories. The *Táin* is a prose-saga with numerous passages of poetry, of which many are in archaic or obscure rhetoric. In the case of the verse passages, Kinsella has tried to follow the sense and structural effects of the original 'with reasonable faithfulness'. In the case of the rhetoric the aim, he says, was 'to produce such passages of verse which more or less match the original for length, ambiguity and obscurity, and which carry the phrases and motifs and occasional short runs that are decipherable in the Irish.... No attempt has been made to follow the Irish verse forms.' (*The Táin*, p. xii).

It is difficult to assess the poetic effects of this poetry out of context, but a few examples may help to suggest the various kinds of poetic utterance involved and the fine vigorous quality of the translation. The following cry of loneliness by the epic-hero, Cuchulainn, as he defends his province against the invading armies is direct and simple in manner:

'I am alone against hordes.
I can neither halt nor let pass.
I watch through the long hours
alone against all men.

Tell Conchobor to come now.
It wouldn't be too soon.
Mágach's sons have stolen our cattle
to divide between them.

> I have held them single-handed,
> but one stick won't make fire.
> Give me two or three
> and torches will blaze!
>
> I am almost worn out
> by single contests.
> I can't kill all their best
> alone as I am.'

(p. 136)

Much of the poetry is in quite a different vein, such as the boasting of heroes. When Cuchulainn engages in single-combat with his boyhood companion Ferdia, he speaks as follows:

Cúchulainn   'You have reached your doom,
          your hour is come.
          My sword will slash
           and not softly.
          When we meet you will fall
          at a hero's hands.
          Never again
           will you lead men.'

(pp. 182-84)

Much of the barbaric splendour of these verbal encounters is lost when read without the magnificence of the context, but Cuchulainn's lament over the dead body of his friend is surprisingly tender after the bravado and carnage that has gone before:

> 'Ferdia of the hosts
> and the hard blows, beloved
> golden brooch, I mourn
> your conquering arm

110

and our fostering together,
a sight to please a prince;
your gold-rimmed shield,
your slender sword,

the ring of bright silver
on your fine hand,
your skill at chess,
your flushed, sweet cheek,
...'

(p.201)

But perhaps the finest poetry comes in the speeches of the Morrigan, the goddess of war, in the bloodthirsty prophecy before the final battle and in her sinister address to the Brown Bull. The first creates an appropriate atmosphere for the great final clash.

'Ravens gnawing
              men's necks
blood spurting
              in the fierce fray
hacked flesh
              battle madness
blades in bodies
              acts of war
after the cloaked one's
              hero heat
in man's shape
              he shakes to pieces
the men of Cruachan
              with hacking blows
war is waged
              each trampling each.
Hail Ulster!
              Woe men of Ireland!
Woe to Ulster!
              Hail men of Ireland!'

(p. 238)

111

CHAPTER 5

But the other is a fine example of Kinsella's use of allusive and ambiguous verse delivered, like so much of this poetry, in a declamatory style:

> 'Dark one are you restless
>> do you guess they gather
> to certain slaughter
>> the wise raven
> groans aloud
> the fair fields that enemies infest
>> ravaging in packs
> learn I discern
>> rich plains
> softly wavelike
>> baring their necks
> greenness of grass
>> beauty of blossoms
> on the plains war
>> grinding heroic
> hosts to dust
>> cattle groans the Badb
> the raven ravenous
>> among corpses of men
> affliction and outcry
>> and war everlasting
> raging over Cuailnge
>> death of sons
> death of kinsmen
>> death death!'

(p. 98)

CONCLUSIONS AND CONTINUITIES

CHAPTER 6

CONCLUSIONS AND CONTINUITIES

Everywhere in Thomas Kinsella's work is the sense of unity of design which is partly conscious in origin, and partly unconscious. Viewed chronologically, the poetry reveals the deepening perceptions of his artistic vision. From the straitened inner and outer landscapes of *Another September* (1958), to the psychological investigations of *Downstream* (1962), the paradoxical faith of *Nightwalker* (1968), the creative myths of *Notes From the Land of the Dead* (1972) and *Finistère* (1972), and the balanced relationships of *New Poems* (1973), he has produced a body of material of unusual range and diversity. But as each new collection appears, its distinction is not only of consistent thematic range and of technical advance, but of dynamic organic relationship with previous material.

Notes From the Land of the Dead, for example, is linked verbally directly with 'Phoenix Park', where its ancestral figures were forecast in the concluding lines, but thematically and stylistically with 'Nightwalker' and the *Wormwood* type of poem. Similarly, *Nightwalker*'s verbal nudity was forecast in 'Mirror in February', the concluding poem of *Downstream*, where 'Chrysalides' and the other poems of the final section also anticipate the directions to be taken in the following volume. In a similar fashion 'Another September' announced the moral concerns that would appear in *Downstream*. 'Landscape and Figure', seemingly so central to *Nightwalker*, where it radiates to all the surrounding poems, is in its identification of death in life and life in death a microcosm of the unifying, discovered faith of *Notes From the Land of*

115

the Dead.

On a smaller scale, the opening lines of 'Phoenix Park' echo the more cryptic second stanza of 'An Outdoor Gallery' in *Another September*; 'Sons of the Brave', an abrasive epigram in 'Moralities', is expanded in 'Nightwalker'; the coalescence of objects and people in 'Shoals Returning' anticipates the metamorphoses of *Notes From the Land of the Dead*; the relationship of man and dog in 'Brothers' resembles that of poet and landscape in 'The Poet Egan O'Rahilly, Homesick in Old Age', where the method of metaphorical interchange is again close to the metamorphosis of other poems; and the reflections on the processes of knowledge in 'Soft Toy' resemble those of 'Worker in Mirror, at His Bench'.

By themselves these echoes and resemblances (and the list could be much expanded) might not be of great significance. But taken in conjunction with the larger unifying concerns of Kinsella's work, they suggest the vitality of its reciprocal inner relationships.

Throughout his work, but more particularly in the first two collections, is the feeling of purpose and determination. The strenuous formulation of 'Baggot Street Deserta', the self-conscious preface and the rigorous ethic of *Wormwood*, even the metaphysical diagram of 'Phoenix Park' have in common a self-driving, partly compulsive quality. Even 'Downstream' and 'A Country Walk' move insistently towards their concluding vision. The designing will of the artist which may be detected in these poems, may also be responsible for the style of poems dealing with the ethic of suffering where the rhetoric, like the suffering, gives the impression of being willed and where the restoration of value is sought by juxtaposition and declaration. In these poems Kinsella tends to transform personality into impersonality, to exclude or limit fluencies of rhythm or verbal colorations and to replace them with dissonances, imperative verbs, formally declarative sentences, moods and generic gestures. He releases his feeling for order by the repudiation of disorder and reveals his desire for love by the repudiation of the losses it inflicts.

CONCLUSIONS

The key idea of acceptance, of rooting in the here and now, first asserted in *Another September*, becomes the motivating force for the explorations of *Downstream* and is then embodied in *Nightwalker* as a concept of human relatedness within an evolutionary, partly deterministic ethic. Eventually, in *Notes From the Land of the Dead*, there is no repudiation; acceptance gains a more flexible stature. Here the discoveries of order come as much from the subconscious as from the deliberate will, as the mockery of the old Faustian self in the introductory poem implies. Now the words themselves contain the sense of positive value so that the terminology of death fuses with the terminology of birth. Significantly too, the assertion of love's nourishing necessity, so central to 'Phoenix Park' and to *Wormwood*, is not made. The trust in the self is more complete. Finally, in *New Poems* a harmonious balance is struck between the tragic vision and the creative response.

As long ago as 'Baggot Street Deserta' Kinsella had sought to counter death's negative hunger with the positive creative hunger of the imagination. For at a level below the questions of erosion, death and the artistic act ,which he had early recognized and accepted as his thematic concerns, lies the more fundamental question of how to have an ongoing, creative response to experience. In its larger patterns and in its coherence of recurrent images, metaphors and references, his poetry embodies a constantly changing and evolving imaginative answer to that question. He is specifically recalled to it by the owl-muse of 'Traveller', as by the girl-muse of 'Westland Row', but it permeates and animates his work as a felt moral pressure.

He began as an isolated artist at a fallow period in Irish literature and shared with his post-war contemporaries a sence of precariousness in the very nature of things. Throughout the twenty-two years of his publishing life, he has remained an isolated, primitive yet sophisticated figure whose struggles with himself and with his material have been little affected or ameliorated by the examples of other writers. Realizing that the chaos of modern life has emerged from human wills, he has sought order and understanding through a complex and detailed exploration of the manifestations of chaos in the world at large, in the natural processes, in the life of his country, and in his own personal life. The manner of that search, as it has been transmitted through his poetry, is uniformly grave and serious, compounded of a feeling of pain and a sense of responsibility. Significantly, it is the isolated figure, or the isolated couple, that appears most frequently in his poetry: the questing artist, the solitary or alienated traveller, the brooding observer. Even the static nature of many of the poems, which seem to absorb the total significance of the setting or the subject, is in keeping with an intense and purposive imagination.

There are no final conclusions. Kinsella's explorations yield brief illuminations in the outer and inner darknesses, for the essence of life, as *Finistère* so powerfully celebrates, lies in continuity. The identification of the 'I' figure in this poem with Amhairgin is a confirmation and a development of the experience of all the previous explorer-narrator-observer figures—of *Downstream*, of 'Nightwalker', of 'A Country Walk', of *Notes From the Land of the Dead*—all of those encounters with the rock, or the darkness, or the chaos of evil, violence and despair. For it is out of these unlikely contexts that Kinsella gains his sense of an other within chaos, of a purpose within the apparently mindless. These are the materials from which he makes his tower, and builds the nest of poetry. In responding to the natural urge of continuity, he is joined in *Finistère* with the elemental motion of the moon, sun, wind, ocean and all creation, and fulfils his destiny. The identification with Amhairgin is an affirmation of that acceptance:

> We drew close together, as one,
> and turned inward, salt chaos
> rolling in silence all around us,
> and listened to our own mouths
> mumbling in the sting of spray:
>   —Ill wind end well

CONCLUSIONS

> mild mother
> on wild water pour peace
> who gave us our unrest
> whom we meet and unmeet
> in whose yearning shadow
> we erect our great uprights
> and settle fulfilled
> and build and are still
> unsettled, ...

'I wrote my first poems', Kinsella once observed, 'partly out of curiosity. I found that I continued to write with increasing seriousness and persistence, poetry rapidly becoming my only significant activity' (note 1). As a whole his work dramatizes one man's varied relationship with a desolating universe in which there are great, if precarious, consolations. The love poems exist as the most concrete evidence of these consolations, but in the overall view of his work it may be said that his poetry is Kinsella's best evidence of the integrity and validity of his informing faith in the imagination.

NOTES

Introduction

1   *Contemporary Authors,* vols. 17-18 (Detroit: Gale Research Company, 1967) p. 263.
2   *Poetry Book Society Bulletin,* March 1958.
3   *Contemporary Authors.*
4   *Poetry Book Society Bulletin,* December 1967.
5   From unpublished autobiographical note (1966).
6   His depressive outlook was alleviated to some degree by his meeting with a few individuals who helped him in his late awakening to poetry, and in particular by his meeting with Eleanor Walsh whom he married in December 1955. Through her 'vitality and brilliance under suffering' he seemed to detect 'a possibility of order, suggestions for a (barely) positive dream' (Ibid.).
7   *Directions* (Illinois Art Education Association, Springfield, Illinois, 1966-67).
8   Ibid.
9   *Davis, Mangan, Ferguson: Tradition and the Irish Writer, writings by W.B. Yeats and Thomas Kinsella* (Dublin: Dolmen Press, 1970) pp. 58-59.
10 Ibid., p. 57.
11 *Poetry Book Society Bulletin,* March 1958.
12 *The Breastplate of Saint Patrick* (1954); *Faeth Fiadha* (1954); *The Sons of Usnach* (1954); *Thirty Three Triads* (1955). (Dublin: Dolmen Press.)
13 *Davis, Mangan, Ferguson,* p. 59.
14 Ibid., pp. 64-65.
15 'Poetry Since Yeats: An Exchange of Views,'
    Tri-Quarterly, No. 4 (1965): 106.
16 Ibid., p. 109.
17 Ibid.
18 I have made some tentative moves in this direction in 'New Voices of the Fifties', in *Poetry in Irish and English*, ed. Seán Lucy (Cork: Mercier Press, 1973).

NOTES

Chapter 1

1   *Poems* (1956) contains a group of love lyrics separated from the main collection as a wedding gift. His earliest poems were published in pamphlet form by Dolmen Press—*The Starlit Eye,* (1952), *Three Sonnets* (1952), *Per Imaginem* (1953).
2   *Poetry Book Society Bulletin,* March 1958.
3   Kinsella, 'The Cretan Glance,' (a review of Kazantzakis' book), *Irish Times,* 4 April 1959, p. 6.
4   Ibid.

Chapter 2

1   *Poetry Book Society Bulletin,* September 1962.
2   Ibid.
3   Ibid.

Chapter 3

1   Peter Orr, ed., *The Poet Speaks* (London: Routledge and Kegan Paul, 1966) pp. 105-109.
2   The poem's epigraph and these quotations are from Crashaw's 'In the Holy Nativity of Our Lord God' *Carmen Deo Nostro* (1652 edition).

Chapter 4

1   R.A.S. Macalister, ed. and trans., *The Book of the Taking of Ireland* (Dublin: Irish Texts Society, 1938).

2 *See* Alwyn and Brinley Rees, *Celtic Heritage, Ancient Tradition in Ireland and Wales* (London: Thames and Hudson, 1961).

3 'Report of the Tribunal appointed to inquire into the events on Sunday, 30th January 1972, which led to loss of life in connection with the procession in Londonderry on that day.' (London: HMSO, 18 April 1972) p. 32.

Chapter 5

1 Unpublished autobiographical note (1966).

BIBLIOGRAPHY

The Starlit Eye. Dublin: Dolmen Press, 1952.
Three Legendary Sonnets. Dublin: Dolmen Press, 1952.
Per Imaginem. Dublin: Dolmen Press, 1953.
The Breastplate of Saint Patrick. Dublin: Dolmen Press, 1954.
Faeth Fiadha. Dublin: Dolmen Press, 1954.
Thirty Three Triads. Dublin: Dolmen Press, 1955.
Death of a Queen. Dublin: Dolmen Press, 1956.
Poems. Dublin: Dolmen Press, 1956.
Another September. Dublin: Dolmen Press, 1958.
Moralities. Dublin: Dolmen Press, 1960.
Poems and Translations. New York: Atheneum, 1961.
The Dolmen Miscellany of Irish Writing; Dublin: Dolmen Press, 1962. [Editor, John Montague; Poetry Editor, Thomas Kinsella.]
Downstream. Dublin: Dolmen Press, 1962.
Wormwood. Dublin: Dolmen Press, 1966.
Nightwalker. Dublin: Dolmen Press, 1967.
Nightwalker and other poems. Dublin: Dolmen Press, 1968.
The Táin. Translated by Thomas Kinsella from the Irish *Táin Bó Cuailnge* (The Cattle Raid of Cooley). Dublin: Dolmen Press, 1969.
Tear. Cambridge, Massachusetts: Pym-Randall Press, 1969.
Butcher's Dozen: A Lesson for the Octave of Widgery. Dublin: Peppercanister 1, 1972.
A Selected Life. Dublin: Peppercanister 2, 1972.
Finistère. Dublin: Cuala Press, 1972.
Notes From the Land of the Dead. Dublin: Cuala Press, 1972.
Notes From the Land of the Dead and Other Poems. New York: Knopf, 1973.
New Poems. Dublin: Dolmen Press, 1973.

BIBLIOGRAPHY

Selected Poems 1956-1968. Dublin: Dolmen Press, 1973.
Vertical Man: a sequel to A Selected Life. Dublin: Pepper-
    canister 3, 1973.
*The Good Fight: a poem for the tenth anniversary of the
    death of John F. Kennedy.* Dublin: Peppercanister 4,
    1973.
One. Dublin: Peppercanister 5, 1974.

For a detailed bibliography of Kinsella's work see *Thomas
    Kinsella. A Bibliography* by Hensley C. Woodbridge,
    Eire-Ireland, Vol. II, No. 2 (Summer 1967).

of references to poems and books by Thomas Kinsella